Toward Speaking Excellence

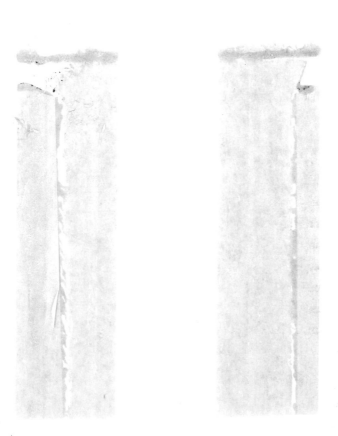

Please note, in September 2003, the Educational Testing Service changed the format of the TSE. Six of the questions included in this book are no longer used on the TSE, and three new questions have been added. This is still a very valuable book to use when preparing for SPEAK test, as that test has not yet changed, but if you are preparing for the TSE, make sure you visit the ETS website to learn about the new changes!

Toward Speaking Excellence

The Michigan Guide to Maximizing Your Performance on the TSE® Test and SPEAK® Test

Dean Papajohn

Ann Arbor

THE UNIVERSITY OF MICHIGAN PRESS

To my parents, Gus and Ethel Papajohn, who encouraged me early on in my education, where I learned to be a good test taker, and

To my wife, Bethany, for helping me retool for a career in TESL.

Acknowledgments

I would like to express my appreciation to all those who helped make this work possible.

First of all, I would like to thank my family—Bethany, Sarah, and Danny—for their enthusiastic support.

I would also like to thank a number of my colleagues at the University of Illinois: Nancy Diamond and Laura Hahn for feedback on early drafts; the staff in the Division of Educational Technologies for their contributions to the artwork; and the staff in the Division of Instructional Development for their input and encouragement.

Of course, thanks go to Kelly Sippell and her team at the University of Michigan Press for advice and help throughout the publishing process.

Contents

Introduction

Who This Book Is For

If you are a nonnative speaker of English, this book is designed to aid you in maximizing your potential on the TSE, the Test of Spoken English, or its institutional counterpart SPEAK, the Speaking Proficiency English Assessment Kit (ETS 1995a). (TSE and SPEAK are registered trademarks of the Educational Testing Service, or ETS. ETS has no connection with this book.) Since the TSE test and the SPEAK test have similar formats, when one test is mentioned in this book, the other one is inferred as well. While this book is written directly to the test taker, ESL instructors will find this book a valuable resource for preparing students for the TSE and SPEAK tests. The materials in this book will also be useful to nonnative speakers at the intermediate to advanced speaking level who are preparing for an oral interview or other oral exams or who desire to improve their communication skills in general.

What This Book Contains

Communication strategies and test-taking strategies for responding to all the sections of the TSE and SPEAK are included in this book. Sample questions and responses provide review and practice. Whether you are using this material as part of an ESL class or workshop or are studying these materials on your own, you will find that this material can help you practice and improve your spoken English as well as assist you in becoming more *test wise* for the new TSE and SPEAK tests.

Test-wiseness allows test takers to utilize knowledge of the test format to their advantage. *Test-wiseness* is considered valuable by many testing experts. The Division of Measurement and Evaluation at the University of Illinois in Champaign–Urbana writes, "Test-wiseness is positive when it allows students to better demonstrate their knowledge of course material" (*Q & A* 1994). They also say of test-wiseness, "since these skills provide a systematic method for completion of a test, students should be encouraged to use them" (*Q & A* 1995). Preparing for tests is an important part of obtaining accurate and fair test scores. "Wider experience and training in preparing for and taking tests of all kinds is likely to increase accuracy of measurement and, therefore, the fairness of scores for the students tested" (Hopkins, Stanley, and Hopkins 1990).

Because the new TSE is based on communicative competence, the communication strategies shared in this book will not only help make you more test wise, but they will arm you with techniques to communicate more clearly. As you learn to package your language in a manner that clearly communicates, you will sound more fluent and in control of your language. Whether you are studying these materials on your own or are an ESL instructor helping to prepare others for the TSE or SPEAK, you will find solid linguistic and test-taking advice and practice within these pages.

How to Use This Book

If you are studying these materials independently, start at the beginning of the book and work your way through. The best test preparation will be done if you start long before your test date arrives. Study one chapter at a time. It's important to actually do the practice exercises because oral communication involves the physical action of speaking as well as the mental formation and organization of ideas. Practice speaking English aloud as much as you can by talking to others or tape-recording yourself. Seek feedback from an ESL instructor if possible and use the knowledge you gain from this book to evaluate recordings of yourself. At the end of each unit there are sets of practice test questions. Don't look at all of these at once. After practicing one set, analyze your responses and determine what you should do to improve before going on to the next set of practice questions. If you look over all the practice questions at once, the spontaneity will be lost. The same holds true for the unofficial practice tests in the appendix. Save these until you have completed the entire book. Then use these practice tests to simulate an actual test by timing yourself and recording your responses. As you read and practice with this material, you will find yourself moving *Toward Speaking Excellence*.

Chapter 1

Preparation Fundamentals for the TSE Test or SPEAK Test

In this chapter you will:

- Consider what makes effective communication;
- Learn how this book is organized;
- Learn the four competencies that define communicative competence for the TSE; and
- Learn general TSE test preparation strategies.

What Makes Effective Communication?

Consider a situation where you had trouble communicating with someone else in English. Describe your experience below, including where you were, who you were speaking with, what you were talking about, and why you had trouble communicating.

_____

_____

_____

_____

_____

_____

Now review the situation you described alone or with a partner and identify communication skills you could have used to better get your meaning across.

_____

_____

_____

_____

_____

_____

_____

Even native speakers of English run into miscommunications, so having strategies to overcome these inevitable communication problems is important. An effective communicator has a storehouse of strategies to communicate different things in different ways, as the situation calls for. Throughout this book you will learn how to effectively communicate in many situations you will face in real life and on the TSE or SPEAK tests.

How This Book is Organized

The TSE (or the new SPEAK) consists of three warm-up questions and twelve rated questions. This book will take you through a practice test question by question. The sample questions used in this book are similar to those published by ETS (ETS 1995b) in their 1995–96 *TOEFL Bulletin*. ETS released these questions to show examinees samples of typical TSE questions so examinees could "become familiar with [the] TSE" before actually taking the test. Information on how to register for the TSE is provided in Appendix B.

In chapter 2 the TSE score levels and scoring criteria are explained, and sample responses at different score levels are presented and discussed. There are five sections to the test, which we will label:

Warm-up section,
Map section,
Picture section,
Graph section, and
Announcement section.

Each of these five sections is discussed in chapters 3–7. Each chapter covers the typical types of questions found in a specific section of the test. You will see sample test questions shown in **bold lettering** surrounded by a single-lined box. The time allotted for the response appears in parentheses following the question. Sample questions look like this:

> **Sample question.** (response time = 60 seconds)

Sample responses in ***bold, italic lettering*** surrounded by a double-lined box follow each question. Sample responses look like this:

> ***Sample response.***

A discussion about how to prepare and deliver an effective oral response along with practice exercises follows each sample response. In addition, at the end of each of these chapters, practice questions have been included to provide you with the opportunity to apply the oral language skills discussed throughout this book. Chapter 8 provides practical test-taking tips for before, during, and after the TSE. Appendix A contains complete sets of unofficial practice tests for further practice.

Four Rating Criteria

Examinees should know the criteria by which they are evaluated. Raters of the TSE focus on four areas of communicative competence. These areas are language function, appropriateness, coherence/cohesion, and accuracy.

> **Language functions** *include recommending, giving directions, giving and defending an opinion, describing, persuading, comparing, defining, announcing, etc.*

Each question focuses on one or more language functions. Since there are many language functions, every test does not include questions with the same language functions. For example, question 3 on one test form may be to give and defend an opinion, while on another test form the question may ask you to compare.

Appropriateness *refers to responding with language appropriate for the intended audience or situation.*
Typically the test will ask you to imagine you are talking to a friend. Sometimes the test specifies that you are talking to someone new to the area, someone without background in your field, a boss, or some specific audience. At other times the test just asks you to "tell the narrator." In this situation you can assume the narrator is a friend; therefore, you can talk as you would to a friend.

Coherence/Cohesion *reflects the ways language is organized (coherence) and how ideas relate to each other (cohesion).*
It is important that your responses are not ambiguous. Opinions and recommendations should be stated clearly. Supporting reasons should clearly connect to the main idea.

Accuracy *includes pronunciation, grammar, fluency, and vocabulary.*
Although there are a number of dialects of English, the standard for the TSE and SPEAK is the English of a university educated person in the United States.

Tips on how to excel in each of these four areas are provided in the discussion of each question/response pair in chapters 3–7.

General Test Preparation Strategies

In order to maximize your performance on the TSE you can prepare in the following ways.

1. Become familiar with the standard directions for the test.
2. Become familiar with typical sample questions for the test.

3. Become familiar with the rating criteria of language functions, appropriateness, coherence/cohesion, and accuracy and how they relate to good responses for test questions.
4. Practice responding to sample questions on your own and within the specific time allotted.

When you take the TSE, the questions are not only given orally from an audiotape but the full questions are shown printed in the test book. As the question is being given orally, you should follow along in the test book. Make sure you understand exactly what the question is asking. If your response does not match the question asked, you may not succeed in the language function or appropriateness of response. Furthermore, by listening carefully to the question, you may hear how to pronounce words or phrases that will be useful to you in your response.

It is best to concentrate on one question at a time. Bring a small watch with a second hand or a digital watch that counts the seconds. This will help you to keep track of your own time as you respond to questions. For instance, if you are running short on time for a particular question, start bringing your response to a conclusion. At the end of the response time for a particular question, you will hear the test narrator say the number of the next test question or begin directions for a new section of the test. If by chance you do poorly on one question, do not let it hinder the remainder of your performance. Put that question behind you and focus your complete concentration on the new question. If you do not finish your response but are clearly on task and accomplishing the language function appropriately, coherently, and accurately, then your score will not be penalized for not finishing the task. However, responses that are incomplete due to lack of organization or lack of vocabulary will not be given maximum scores.

As much as you can, put the testing environment out of your mind. If your test is given in a language laboratory with a lot of other people, be prepared to hear a buzz of noise when everyone is responding. Always take a few seconds to think about your response before responding, even if other people begin responding immediately. Likewise, if you finish a few seconds before the allotted time is up, don't worry if other people are still speaking. To help you ignore noise in the testing environment, try to respond to the questions as if you were talking to someone sitting across from you. Concentrate on talking with this person as if you really desired to communicate that specific information. If instead, you are thinking in the back of your mind how awful it is to be taking this test, it probably will show up negatively in the way you respond. On the other hand, if you put enthusiasm into your voice, your intonation will reflect it and you will be seeking ways to effectively communicate your thoughts. Remember, the actual TSE test time is only around 20 minutes, so it is important to maximize your speaking performance during that time. The sample questions and responses that follow will help you to do your best when you take the TSE.

Chapter 2
Test Scoring

In this chapter you will:

- Learn about the scoring scale used for the TSE;
- Learn how the scoring scale relates to the four communicative competencies; and
- See example responses at various score levels and learn why they were scored at that particular level.

Scoring Scale

The TSE scores range from 20 to 60 in 5 point increments. Therefore, possible scores include 20, 25, 30, 35, 40, 45, 50, 55, and 60. You should not worry that you have to speak like a native speaker of English to receive a score of 60. Since the TSE was designed for nonnative speakers of English, a native speaker of English would be expected to score well beyond a 60 if higher scores could be given (ETS 1996). Therefore, a high score on the TSE is not out of reach of a nonnative speaker of English.

There is no universal passing score for the TSE. Different institutions, whether they are universities or licensing boards, are responsible for setting their own passing or cutoff scores (ETS 1996), so you should check with your institution to find out the score you need. If you take the TSE, ETS will rate your tape and report your scores to you and to the institutions you indicated when you registered for the test. If you take the SPEAK, the institution that gave you the test will rate your test tape and report your score. Even though ETS does not rate SPEAK tests, institutions administering the SPEAK use ETS guidelines (ETS 1996) for scoring. Institutions do not generally report SPEAK scores to other institutions, whereas TSE scores can be reported to all institutions by ETS.

Communicative Competencies and Scoring

Each even numbered score has a description that relates to overall communication ability in general and language function, appropriateness, coherence/cohesion, and accuracy specifically. A summary of the rating scale is shown below (ETS 1996).

Level 60

A score of 60 indicates that the response almost always communicates well. That means language functions are addressed well. Furthermore, the language chosen is appropriate for the audience and context, is coherent and cohesive, and is linguistically accurate. Linguistic errors may be present, but do not interfere with the message.

Level 50

A score of 50 indicates that the response usually communicates well. That means language functions are usually addressed well. Furthermore, the language chosen is usually appropriate for the audience and context, is coherent and usually cohesive, and is usually linguistically accurate. Any linguistic errors usually do not interfere with the message.

Level 40

A score of 40 indicates that the response partially communicates. That means language functions are partially addressed. Furthermore, the language chosen is kind of appropriate for the audience and context, is kind of coherent and kind of cohesive, and is only sometimes linguistically accurate. Linguistic errors may interfere with the message.

Level 30

A score of 30 indicates that the response usually does not communicate well. That means language functions are usually not addressed well. Furthermore, the language chosen is usually not appropriate for the audience and context, is usually incoherent and usually noncohesive, and is usually not linguistically accurate. Linguistic errors usually do interfere with the message.

Level 20

A score of 20 indicates that the response does not communicate well. That means language functions are not addressed well. Furthermore, the language chosen is not appropriate for the audience and context, is incoherent and noncohesive, and is not linguistically accurate. Linguistic errors interfere with the message.

In general terms the score levels have the following meanings. A score of 60 indicates that you are always understood by the rater and that the rater does not have to apply extra effort in understanding you. A score of 50 means that you are generally understandable, even though there are errors. Both 50 and 60 are positive scores, because communication has been successful. A score of 40 is the middle-of-the-road score, sometimes positive, sometimes negative. At times, a person scoring 40 is understandable, but at other times the rater has difficulty understanding what was said. That is, the rater must apply effort to understand a person scoring 40. A score of 30 means that although the examinee has responded, not much of what was said addresses the task or makes sense. A score of 20 means the rater doesn't really understand what the examinee is trying to communicate. Both 20 and 30 are negative scores, because ideas are not communicated clearly. While raters only assign each question an even score of 20, 30, 40, 50, or 60, final scores of 25, 35, 45, and 55 may occur. Final scores are based on the average of the twelve test questions and the rounded average between two raters.

Sample Responses

Now let's take a look at a typical question and some sample responses that represent different score levels.

> **Imagine that we are classmates from college. I came to visit you at your home during break. Suggest one place in town you think I should go to see while I am visiting your town and justify your recommendation with reasons.**
> (response time = 30 seconds)

Response scored at 60

> *Well, I know you have an interest in architecture. Therefore I recommend that you visit our town's historical society. They have a special exhibit about the architecture in our city. In the exhibit you will see photographs and models of various buildings of architectural significance in our city. I know you especially like seeing old blueprints and they have plenty of those on display. You can easily spend a couple of hours viewing those exhibits.*

The language function is clearly carried out; that is, the Historical Society is *recommended* because of the special architecture exhibit. The language appropriately takes into account the audience. The friend's interest in architecture in general, and in blueprints specifically, is addressed. Expressions like *well, plenty of, a couple of,* are informal and appropriate when speaking with a friend. The response is nicely organized because it begins with acknowledging the friend's interest in architecture, goes on to relate that to the Historical Society's architecture exhibit, and concludes with an estimate of how long it will take to view the exhibit. This response demonstrates good vocabulary such as *architectural significance* and *blueprints.* If this response were spoken fluently, with natural English rhythm, stress, and intonation, then it should receive a score of 60.

Response scored at 50

> *Our city is famous for its museums. The best one . . . One of my favorite ones are the Historical Society. I like the architecture exhibit. I think you would like it. The admission price . . . It only costs about $3.00 for admission. They gave you a free map of an architectural walking tour. So after learning about the buildings you can take a tour. I mean follow the map and see these great buildings for yourself.*

Again the language function is clearly carried out; that is, the Historical Society is *recommended* because of the architecture exhibit. In fact a second recommendation is made, that is, to take the walking tour. Making two recommendations does not in itself earn the speaker a higher score, but it does indicate that the speaker can communicate his ideas in a reasonable amount of time. Although the friend's interests are not taken into account as directly as in the level 60 response, the speaker does suggest that the friend will enjoy it because he himself enjoys it. The response is organized simply. It begins with museums in general, narrows to the Historical Society, and focuses on the architecture exhibit. Concrete examples like the $3.00 admission price and the walking tour map help to communicate the speaker's ideas. This response contains simple sentence structure and vocabulary such as *I like . . .* instead of the more complex *I have always been fascinated by . . . .* Although this phrasing is simple, it is appropriate. Notice that the speaker begins sentences and then starts over with an alternative phrasing. While this reduces fluency it is not a major error that interferes with the communication. Also, the speaker mentions a tour and then, to clear up confusion, clarifies that it is a self-directed tour. There are a few grammar errors in verb tense, such as *my favorite ones are . . .* instead of *is* and *They gave you . . .* instead of *give.* Imagine that the speaker pronounced some of his vowels incorrectly on words like *famous, cost, tour,* and *follow* yet was generally understandable. If this response were otherwise spoken fluently, with natural English rhythm, stress, and intonation, then it should receive a score of 50.

Response scored at 40

> *Yes, there are a building . . . a museum building. uh This building is, uh, the Historic Societ. At this building , uh, there are the architecture exhibit. You will be interesting to see. There are pictures, uh, photos, uh, drawing, uh you know, of all the interesting buildings in my , uh city. OK? It is open until 5 p.m. You will be interesting to see.*

This type of response represents the middle-of-the-road answer, sometimes communicative, sometimes unclear. The language function of recommending with reasons is accomplished, but only after some effort. The speaker tries to consider his audience by suggesting that the friend will find the exhibit interesting, but the audience appropriateness is weakened by the awkward grammar and wording. There is little cohesion between sentences; along with the pausing and *uh* sounds, this makes for a choppy response. There are simple grammar errors like *there is/are a building* . . . and *interested/ing*. Pronunciation is difficult to understand with the chopping off of word endings such as *Historical, Society,* and *drawings*. This response should be rated 40.

Response scored at 30

> *OK, you would, uh, like, uh, to visit, uh, my hometown. OK, OK, uh, my hometown is, uh, a big city. There is, uh, uh, a lot to do . . . in my , my city. Like museums.*

In this response the language function is only minimally carried out. While the speaker says her hometown is a big city and that there is a lot to do, she does not recommend visiting a specific place for specific reasons. Only at the end is the vague expression *museums* hastily mentioned. Because the speaker does not say much, the raters are not able to clearly assess whether the speaker is able to address the specific audience of a college classmate appropriately. The response is short, which also makes it difficult to rate coherence and cohesion. Content and details are lacking from this response. Sentences are short and of simple construction; the last phrase is not even a complete sentence. The unnecessary repetition of *OK* and the sound *uh* interfere with fluency and rhythm. Even if this response were spoken with good stress and intonation, it should be scored at 30.

Responses scored at 20

> *Suggest some place I should plan to see . . .*

This response is only the repetition of part of the question. The speaker does not create any language to be rated and therefore should be scored 20.

> *When you visit . . . I think you would like to see . . . In my hometown . . . Many places you visit.*

This response does not address the language function of recommending with reasons; it does not address audience appropriateness; the incomplete sentences make it highly incoherent; and the fluency, rhythm, and vocabulary are weak. Therefore a score of 20 should be assigned to this response as well.

It is important always to give some kind of response to each question. If you do not say anything at all or say something like, "Sorry, I don't know," then the raters will have no choice but to assign a score of 20 to that response. No matter what, it is important to respond to all of the questions.

On the other hand, don't become upset if you don't give your best response to every question. There are twelve questions that will be averaged into your final score. So concentrate on each question as it is asked. The next chapters will provide you with advice and practice on how to maximize your communication abilities throughout the test.

Chapter 3
Warm-up Section

In this chapter you will:

- Learn about the purpose of the warm-up section of the TSE;
- See examples of warm-up questions and responses;
- Learn what makes an effective response to warm-up questions; and
- Practice responding to practice warm-up questions.

The general directions for the warm-up section of the test will be similar to this:

> **This test begins with a few simple questions about familiar things. These are warm-up questions to help you get ready for the main test questions. However, your warm-up responses will not be listened to by the raters. Do your best to give complete answers to each of these questions.**

While the warm-up section of the TSE is not rated, it is an important part of the test. Although raters are instructed not to listen to this section of the test, it provides you with an opportunity to warm up your voice and to become comfortable speaking into the recording equipment. Since you cannot be 100% sure that a rater will not listen to or stumble onto this section, try to do your best from the start. By starting off strong on the warm-up section, you will build up your confidence and be more at ease during the remainder of the test. On the other hand, if you mumble or falter on an answer during the warm-up, don't worry about it. The whole point is to prepare you. It's better to release your nervousness during the warm-up section so you can do your best on the rated portion of the TSE.

There are three simple and straightforward questions in this section of the test. Since you will only have 10 seconds to answer each question, your answers should be simple and straightforward as well. Do not try to say too much; the more you say the more chance you have to mispronounce sounds and confuse the raters if they happen to listen. Try to say enough to answer the question without ambiguity. By doing so, you will demonstrate that you know how to say what you want to say, and thus build up your confidence.

3a. Warm-up Section, Question 1

The first question of the warm-up section may be similar to:

> **What is the test number on the label of your test tape?**
> (response time = 10 seconds)

When you respond to this question, give a short, complete sentence. You may even want to repeat the number for clarity. For a tape number of 4320, an example response would be:

> *The number is four thousand three hundred and twenty, four-three-two-zero.*

Although this response is short, it sounds fluent because it answers the question directly in a complete sentence and focuses on the important information.

Exercise 3.1

To further prepare for this section, practice saying numbers by counting from:

0 to 10 by ones,
10 to 100 by tens,
100 to 1000 by hundreds, and
1000 to 10,000 by thousands.

Note that when pronouncing *thousand* you should use a voiceless /th/ sound as in *thin, think,* and *theory.*

Exercise 3.2

When a noun does not follow a number, the primary stress goes on the last stressed syllable (see Dickerson and Hahn 1998). For example, in 8347 the first syllable of *seven (sev)* is given primary stress. Practice saying the four-digit numbers listed below. Be sure to place the stress on the underlined part:

8347	9752	3972	5689	2780	4193
7248	6556	3327	2050	5948	8288
2190	1643	6191	3801	4824	7899

The first question frequently asks about the number on the test booklet. So you should be prepared for that specific question in case it is asked. When you first receive your test book, make sure you locate the number on the cover of the test book. Use the brief time before the test begins to think about how to say the identification number. Pronounce it to yourself silently. In this way you will be prepared for the first question even before it is asked. This will increase your confidence and help you maximize your speaking performance.

3b. Warm-up Section, Question 2

The second question of the warm-up section may be similar to:

> **When did you begin studying English?**
> (response time = 10 seconds)

The TSE is supposed to measure the *way* you say your answer, not the actual answer. Yet raters are human, so it is important to make a good impression on the rater from the beginning. Therefore, you should speak confidently and fluently to communicate your response to the given question. As before, when you respond to this question, give a short, complete sentence. It is not essential to give the exact amount of time in months or years. You can use words like *almost* and *approximately* to qualify your answer. An example response is:

> *I began studying English approximately 5 years ago.*

Often it is helpful to use the stem of the question to begin your answer. For example, the question asks, *When did you begin . . .* so the answer starts off with *I began . . . .* This helps to produce responses that are complete sentences in a prompt and fluent manner.

You don't need to elaborate on your answer by explaining whether you have studied English in school or on your own or whether you have studied in your home country or in the United States. Additional information could adversely affect the rater's judgment of you, so be careful about supplying information that is not specifically asked for in the question. By trying to add additional information in your response you increase the opportunity for errors. Likewise, you may find it hard to finish in 10 seconds and end up being cut off. This will likely result in sounding incoherent. In contrast, a short, complete answer sounds fluent and shows that you are in control of your language.

Exercise 3.3

Now look below at ten different responses to this question. Decide which you think are the five best responses and place a check mark by them. Compare your check marks with a partner. Discuss what you liked about the responses you checkmarked and how you could improve the responses you didn't mark.

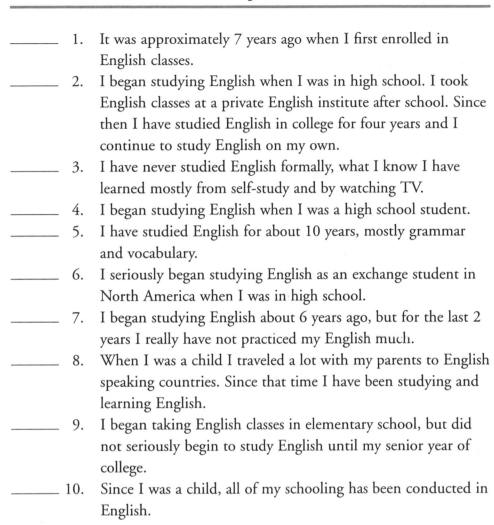

_____ 1. It was approximately 7 years ago when I first enrolled in English classes.

_____ 2. I began studying English when I was in high school. I took English classes at a private English institute after school. Since then I have studied English in college for four years and I continue to study English on my own.

_____ 3. I have never studied English formally, what I know I have learned mostly from self-study and by watching TV.

_____ 4. I began studying English when I was a high school student.

_____ 5. I have studied English for about 10 years, mostly grammar and vocabulary.

_____ 6. I seriously began studying English as an exchange student in North America when I was in high school.

_____ 7. I began studying English about 6 years ago, but for the last 2 years I really have not practiced my English much.

_____ 8. When I was a child I traveled a lot with my parents to English speaking countries. Since that time I have been studying and learning English.

_____ 9. I began taking English classes in elementary school, but did not seriously begin to study English until my senior year of college.

_____ 10. Since I was a child, all of my schooling has been conducted in English.

3c. Warm-up Section, Question 3

The third question of the warm-up section may be similar to:

Why did you decide to learn to speak English?
(response time = 10 seconds)

When responding, do not wander from the question and do not supply information that is not asked for. As with warm-up question 2, you do not want to adversely affect the raters' opinions of you if they happen to listen in. Do not indicate whether this is the first or the fifth time you are taking the TSE. Although raters are trained to focus on how you speak and not be influenced by the content of your response, raters don't need to know if other raters have scored you low in the past and caused you to retake the test. Also, be careful to frame your response in a positive way rather than a negative way. Do not tell the rater you are forced to take this test by your university or that you are afraid you will not get a certain job if you don't pass the test. Respond in a positive way, for example:

> *I plan to study at an American university.*

or

> *I learned English so I can communicate with scholars around the world.*

This type of response communicates confidence and directly answers the question asked. Short, complete answers convey fluency and control of language.

3d. Warm-up Section, Practice Questions

These practice questions will help you prepare to think quickly and respond concisely to warm-up section questions. Work on one practice set at a time. Reading all the questions at once will ruin the spontaneity of your responses. Make your practice as realistic as possible by not looking ahead at other questions and by keeping the time limit. For each set of questions below, tape-record your responses. Then listen to each response to see if you have answered concisely, fluently, and in a positive manner. Correct and repeat responses that need improvement before going on to the next practice set.

Practice Set 1

- What is your social security number?
  (response time = 10 seconds)
- How long have you been waiting for the test to begin?
  (response time = 10 seconds)
- Why did you bring a watch with you?
  (response time = 10 seconds)

Practice Set 2

- What is your telephone number?
  (response time = 10 seconds)
- How long did it take you to get to the test center?
  (response time = 10 seconds)
- Why did you decide to wear those clothes today?
  (response time = 10 seconds)

Practice Set 3

- What is your driver's license number?
  (response time = 10 seconds)
- How long have you owned your watch?
  (response time = 10 seconds)
- Why did you leave your calculator at home today?
  (response time = 10 seconds)

Remember, the warm-up section is not rated, so use it to get off to a good start for the remainder of the test.

Chapter 4
Map Section

In this chapter you will:

- Become familiar with the instructions for questions 1, 2, and 3 of the TSE;
- See examples of questions 1, 2, and 3 and corresponding responses;
- Learn what makes an effective response to questions 1, 2, and 3; and
- Practice responding to practice questions 1, 2, and 3.

The general directions for the map section of the test will be similar to this:

> **That finishes the warm-up questions and now on to the rated part of the test. For each question, try to communicate your thoughts to the rater in a complete and understandable manner.**
>
> **For the next few questions try to pretend that we are classmates from college. We are looking at a map of your hometown together, a town where I have never been before. Please look over the map for the next half of a minute. After that you will be asked the questions written below.**

In this section you will be shown a map that will be used as the context for the next three questions. Pay close attention to the context. Is the map of a place that is supposed to be new to you, or is it supposed to be of a place you are familiar with, like your hometown? Are you speaking to someone who has been to this place before, or is it new to this person? What is your relationship to the person you are speaking with? Should you speak in a formal or an informal manner? It is important to evaluate the context in order to score well on the appropriateness of your language.

You will be given 30 seconds to study the map. Use this time wisely. During those 30 seconds you should look over the names of the streets, buildings, and other landmarks. Practice pronouncing those names that look difficult to you. Generally longer words and words with consonant clusters will be more challenging to pronounce.

There are a number of common themes for street names used throughout cities in the United States. These themes include numbers, presidents, states, and trees. English has a number of words that are used in formal street names besides the ending *Street*. These include Road, Avenue, Drive, Way, Boulevard, Circle, and Court. The primary stress on street names depends on whether it has the ending *Street* or not. Street names with the ending *Street* carry primary stress on the word before *Street* (see Dickerson and Hahn 1998). In the following street names the underlined word carries the primary stress: First Street, Washington Street, and Oak Street. For street names using endings other than *Street,* the primary stress goes on the ending. For example, in the following street names the underlined word carries the primary stress: Fifth Avenue, Wilson Road, and Riverside Drive.

Exercise 4.1

Lists of street names are shown in categories on pages 27 and 28. It is useful to practice pronouncing some street names before the test. Look at a map of your own town or a town you plan to visit in the United States and find three additional street names to add to each of the lists below. Practice saying aloud each of the street names from the list. Look back over the list

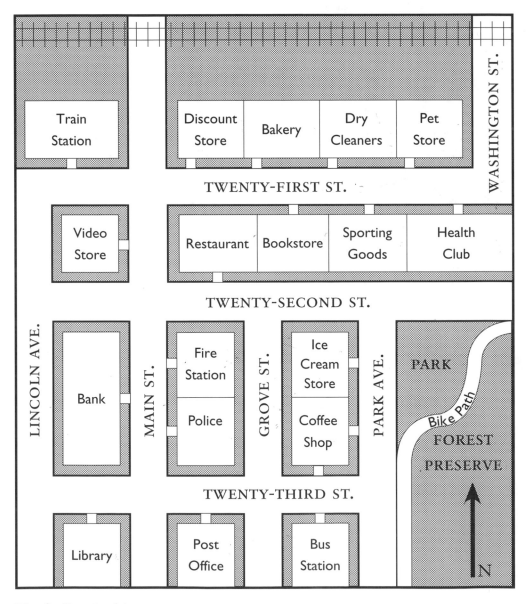

Map for Exercise 4.1

and put a check mark by the ten street names that are hardest for you to pronounce. Repeat these ten aloud for extra practice and ask a native speaker of English to listen and correct your pronunciation if necessary.

Number streets generally use ordinal numbers like:

First Street   Tenth Street
Second Street   Twentieth Street
Third Street   Twenty-First Street
Fourth Street

_____

_____

_____

Common presidential streets include:

Washington Street   Roosevelt Road
Lincoln Avenue   Wilson Road
Jefferson Street

_____

_____

_____

Common state streets include:

Ohio Street   California Street
Illinois Street   Pennsylvania Avenue

_____

_____

_____

Common tree streets include:

Oak Street   Pine Street
Elm Street   Maple Street

_____

_____

_____

Other common U.S. street names include:

State Street   Franklin Road
Main Street   Park Avenue
Prospect Avenue   Riverside Drive

_____

_____

_____

During your time to study the map, also observe the compass directions of north, south, east, and west. Notice if there are any rivers, lakes, parks, and railroad tracks. Then look over the map and pick one place that you are familiar with and could talk about. Think of vocabulary that is associated with that place. For example, if you pick the post office, think of vocabulary that would be useful in describing it, like: stamps, letters, packages, long lines, overnight express, mail, ship, send, and deliver.

Exercise 4.2

For each of the places listed on p. 29, think of and list between five to ten words or phrases related to that place. Remember to include nouns, verbs, adjectives, and adverbs if possible.

Library

_____

_____

_____

_____

_____

_____

_____

_____

_____

Bank

_____

_____

_____

_____

_____

_____

_____

_____

_____

Bookstore

_____

_____

_____

_____

_____

_____

_____

_____

_____

Health Club

_____

_____

_____

_____

_____

_____

_____

_____

Pet Store

_____

_____

_____

_____

_____

_____

_____

_____

Discount Store

_____

_____

_____

_____

_____

_____

_____

_____

4a. Map Section, Question 1

Question 1 may be similar to this:

> **Imagine that we are classmates from college. I came to visit you at your home during break, but you got sick after I arrived. Suggest one place in town you think I should go on my own and justify your recommendation with reasons.**
> (response time = 30 seconds)

Although only 30 seconds is allotted for the response to this question, it is wise to take a few seconds to organize your thoughts. Since this sample question asks you to provide reasons, try to give more than one reason. For example, if you recommend the ice cream store, you might mention the large variety of flavors, the natural ingredients, and the low prices. Don't try to think of too many reasons because you will either waste time or rush to say everything you want to say. On the other hand, if you can only think of one reason, that is alright as long as you clearly explain your one reason. Frame your response in a way that will help the rater understand what you say; this includes previewing your reasons, providing details, and concluding. Speaking in this manner communicates that you are a clear thinker with the ability to communicate your thoughts in words. In other words, it sounds like you are in control of your language rather than just speaking haphazardly off the top of your head. Furthermore, because you have a solid strategy for responding to questions, you can speak more confidently. Here is a sample response:

> *I think you really ought to go to the ice cream store. I know you'll enjoy it for three important reasons!*
>
> *First of all, they have a variety of flavors, over 100 different kinds! Second, all their ice cream is made with natural ingredients. No preservatives or artificial flavors are used. But best of all are the low prices!*
>
> *I know you like a choice of healthy, inexpensive treats, so the ice cream store is definitely a place you'll want to go!*

The exclamation points emphasize the need to speak enthusiastically. Since you have been asked to role-play, you want your recommendation to sound convincing. Enthusiasm will help you put the needed intonation in your voice. Enthusiasm also tends to lower your anxiety level, which in turn lets you communicate to your maximum potential.

Since this context presents two college classmates talking, informal language is appropriate. Notice the use of contractions like *you'll.* Also notice the familiarity expressed in phrases like *I think you really ought to . . . , I know you'll enjoy it . . . ,* and *I know you like a . . . .* Rhythm can also be enhanced by using reduced forms like *oughta* for *ought to* and *wanna* for *want to.*

The response is divided into three parts: preview, details, and conclusion. The preview is just two short sentences. Its purpose is to introduce the topic and clue the rater about what to listen for. The topic is clearly the ice cream store, and the rater is guided to listen for three key reasons. United States listeners expect to be guided in their listening in this way. So if you don't guide your rater, you will make him or her work harder to understand you.

The middle four sentences give the details one by one. Transitions and markers are used to highlight the key ideas: *First of all . . . , Second . . . ,* and *But best of all . . . .* Details are given to make the ideas concrete. Variety is described as *over 100 different kinds,* and the term *natural ingredients* is explained as *no preservatives or artificial flavors.* The response time is short, so avoid talking about ideas that are abstract because abstract ideas are hard to describe and explain.

The conclusion in this response is only one sentence, but it is an important part of the answer because it summarizes the main ideas with the words *choice, healthy,* and *inexpensive.* At the end of the allotted response time, you will hear the narrator say the number of the next test question followed by directions for the next question. If you keep speaking about your reasons until after the narrator goes on to the next question, it might sound as if you don't know how to concisely answer the question. If you do run out of time, rather than stop midsentence you should finish up your sentence, but don't say more than a few words after the response time has ended. However, by watching your time and including a short summary within the allotted time, you demonstrate that you are in control of your thoughts and your language. The summary keeps the main ideas in the rater's mind, so the raters find it easier to recall your main points and thereby conclude you have accomplished the intended language function. This gives a positive impression of your communication skills.

One common mistake made by test takers is to merely give a list of places to go as in the response below.

> *It would be nice to go to the ice cream store, or you might want to go to the discount store, or the bakery is nearby, or the bookstore. The sporting goods store is another place or the health club next door. The other place you could go is the library.*

This type of response, even if spoken fluently, will be scored low because it does not give any reasons for visiting any of these places.

Exercise 4.3

This exercise is for additional practice on generating ideas quickly about different places. Place a check mark by one of the five places listed below and write a short paragraph about it. After writing your paragraph, close your book and describe the same place aloud in order to work on fluency.

_____ a crowded supermarket

_____ a picnic in the mountains

_____ a championship basketball game

_____ a classroom on the day of the final exam

_____ a computer lab at a university

_____

_____

_____

_____

_____

_____

_____

4b. Map Section, Question 2

Question 2 may be similar to this:

> **I like movies and I would like to pick up a movie at the video store for us to watch. Could you please give me directions from the coffee shop to the video store?**
>
> (response time = 30 seconds)

During the time given to review the map, you already noted the compass directions of north, south, east, and west. You may choose to use these compass directions, or you may say up, down, left, and right. Whichever form of directions you choose, be consistent. Don't switch back and forth from *north* to *up* to *east,* etc. If you identified any street names that you don't feel confident in pronouncing, try to avoid them if possible. If you must use these words, pronounce them slowly, enunciating each syllable. For specifying distance on a city map you can use the term *blocks*. Since you need a few seconds to locate these two places on the map, don't expect to talk for the whole 30 seconds. Remember your role, the context, and your relationship to the speaker. You may also want to refer to other landmarks as you describe the way to go. Here is a sample response:

> *Exit the coffee shop onto Twenty-Third Street between Park Avenue and Grove Street. Walk west on Twenty-Third Street for one and a half blocks. At Twenty-Third and Main, turn north. On the second block you'll see a large restaurant on the east side of the street. On the west side, across from the restaurant, is the video store.*

In this example you are talking to a classmate who has probably never been to your hometown before. Referring to landmarks like *across from the restaurant . . .* is appropriate language to use in this context. Clear directions are important for someone who is new in town. For example, if the starting place is on a corner, be sure to specify which street you are starting on. Also look for indications of doorways or entrances to know where to start and finish. It's important to specify exactly where you are beginning your directions. Otherwise you risk confusing your rater from the start. Look for the most direct route. There are other ways to get to the video store from the coffee shop, but all of these require more streets and more turns. Some people can finish responding to this question before the 30 second time limit. If you finish the task clearly and concisely with time remaining, don't feel pressured to add more to your response because this may cause you to make mistakes or sound unorganized. A simple, concise answer will communicate clearly to the rater and will reduce the opportunity for errors and confusion.

Here is another good alternative response. Think about what makes this set of directions clear.

> *OK, you want to get from the coffee shop to the video store. From the coffee shop take Twenty-Third Street west. Pass Grove Street and then turn right on Main Street. The first street you come to is Twenty-Second Street. Crossing Twenty-Second Street you will see the video store on the left. There's a large neon sign in the window.*

Exercise 4.4

An important part of giving directions is using appropriate pausing. In the response above, put a slash (/) at each place you would pause. Now say the directions in the response above out loud while using appropriate pausing. Ask a native speaker of English to give you feedback on your pausing and pace.

Exercise 4.5

For additional practice, write out directions from your home to the grocery store for an older uncle who has come to visit you. Remember to provide accurate directions and include significant landmarks. Review your directions and insert a slash (/) where you think it is appropriate to pause. Practice giving your directions aloud.

_____

_____

_____

_____

_____

4c. Map Section, Question 3

Question 3 may be similar to this:

> **Imagine that after coming back from the video store I show you the title of the video I picked out. You've already seen this video and it happens to be one of the best videos you've ever seen. Because you're thrilled about this video, you tell me about it and explain the reasons why you find it interesting.**
> (response time = 60 seconds)

You may have many favorite videos; don't take a long time debating with yourself about which one you should discuss. Pick a video that will be easy for you to talk about. This could be a video you have seen recently so the story is fresh in your mind, or it could be a video you enjoy so it is still vivid in your memory. If you have never seen a video or can't remember the last time you have seen a movie, pick a favorite book to talk about and pretend that it has been made into a video.

Notice that the question has two parts. First they ask you to talk about the video and then they ask you to explain why you think it's interesting. As with question 1 in this chapter, give your answer in the form of preview, details, and conclusion. If you try to talk about the plot of the story and then give the reasons you like it, you are probably going to run out of time. Therefore, give the reasons you like the video by giving examples from the video. In this way you will be able to describe part of the video and the reasons you find it interesting at the same time. With this approach you are much more likely to complete your answer in the time allotted. Be sure to keep your comments short and to the point. Think of one or two reasons why you like this story; you probably won't have time to talk about more than that. Keep your reasons short but make them concrete so they will be easily understood by the rater. If you are talking about a movie the rater has never seen and your explanation is vague and rambling, your rating will suffer.

Since this is a video you like, be enthusiastic. In the conclusion encourage the listener to watch this video. Remember that enthusiasm will help you put the needed intonation in your voice and will help lower your anxiety level, which in turn lets you communicate to your maximum potential. Here is a sample response:

> *One of my favorite videos is* **It's A Wonderful Life!** *There are two main reasons why I like this fascinating story.*
>
> *The first reason I like this video is because it shows how the decisions and actions of one person's life can affect many other lives! For example, when George was a boy he jumped into the broken ice of a pond to save his younger brother. George's brother later grew up to be a pilot in the Air Force and saved the lives of many American soldiers. If George hadn't saved his brother when he was a kid, his brother couldn't have saved those soldiers! The other reason I like this video is because it's shown on TV every year at Christmas time. It has become a tradition to watch it every year.*
>
> *If you haven't seen* **It's A Wonderful Life!** *I highly recommend it. It's an interesting story that shows us how closely our lives are tied to each other's. Who knows, you may start your own tradition of watching it every year!*

The above answer starts out by identifying the movie and clueing the rater that there are two key reasons for liking it. The middle part gives details about the story and the reasons for liking it. Each reason is introduced with a transition statement or marker: *The first reason . . . , The other reason . . . .* Enough details are shared to give the rater an idea of the plot but not so many details that the speaker strays from directly answering the question. Pronouns are avoided in specific places in order to eliminate confusion. So instead of saying *He later grew up to be a pilot . . . ,* the speaker says, *George's brother later grew up to be a pilot . . . .* That way there is no confusion about who is the pilot. When making comparisons or contrasts make sure the primary phrase stress reflects this focus. (See Dickerson and Hahn 1998 for more information on how to use phrase stress for comparison and contrast.) For example, in the following sentence the underlined words are being compared and should therefore carry primary stress. *If George hadn't saved his brother when he was a kid, his brother couldn't have saved those soldiers! George* and *brother* are being compared to *brother* and *soldiers.* Since you communicate by how you say something as well as by what you say, be sure to place appropriate stress within a phrase. The final two sentences conclude the answer with a brief summary and an encouragement to watch this movie. Notice exclamation points throughout as reminders to let your intonation show your enthusiasm for the movie. Other markers that communicate enthusiasm are expressions like . . . *fascinating story* and . . . *I highly recommend it.*

Another approach to answering this question would be to talk about the director or the stars rather than the plot.

This is a video of one of my favorite movies, **It's a Wonderful Life!** *Both the directing and the acting in this classic film are superb!*

This is one of the better known films directed by the famous director Frank Capra. In this video, Capra shows how a kindhearted individual can triumph over evil in the world. Capra depicts life in small town America through the depression and World War II in such a way that you feel like you are really living it. The acting is great too. Jimmy Stewart plays the lead role of George Bailey in such a natural way. Stewart beautifully portrays the conflict between dreams and responsibility in this part. Donna Reed also does an excellent job of starring as George's wife.

I think you'll be glad that you saw this memorable video with me.

Exercise 4.6

Now think of a video you have seen and tape-record yourself while you pretend to tell a friend about why you did or did not find it interesting. After recording your response, listen to your tape and evaluate how well you:

- introduced the name of the video;
- clearly stated your opinion, whether you like or don't like this video;
- used specific examples;
- used transitions;
- related your explanation to your audience; and
- used appropriate intonation.

4d. Map Section, Practice Questions

These practice questions will help you prepare to think quickly and respond concisely to map section questions. You should study the appropriate map before answering the questions. Work on one practice set at a time. If you preview all the questions at once, you will ruin the spontaneity. Make your practice as realistic as possible by not looking ahead at other questions and by keeping the time limit. For each set of questions below, tape-record your responses. Then listen to each response to see if you have accurately responded to the specific language function and if you have structured your answer in an easy-to-follow manner. Correct and repeat responses that need improvement.

Practice Set 1 (refer to Map 1)

Imagine I am your coworker visiting you from out of town.

- There are plans for a new fast food restaurant to be built in town. What are some reasons a person might like to go there?
  (response time = 30 seconds)
- I'm getting hungry. Please tell me how to get from the park to the restaurant.
  (response time = 30 seconds)
- It's a sunny day and you are taking a walk in the park. Please tell me about the activities you see taking place at the park. Justify with reasons why this park is beneficial to this town.
  (response time = 60 seconds)

Practice Set 2 (refer to Map 1)

Imagine I am your supervisor at work and we are talking during coffee break.

- Coffee shops have become popular places. What are some of the reasons people like to go to coffee shops?
  (response time = 30 seconds)
- I need to buy some food for my pet. Please give me directions from the coffee shop to the pet store.
  (response time = 30 seconds)
- You just stopped at the pet store last night. Recommend an animal you think would make a good pet. Give reasons to justify your recommendation.
  (response time = 60 seconds)

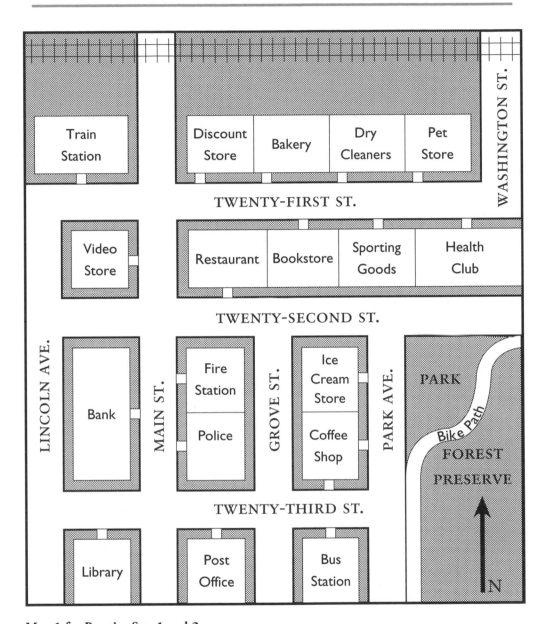

Map 1 for Practice Sets 1 and 2

Practice Set 3 (refer to Map 2)

Imagine we're classmates from college and I came for a visit in your hometown.

- Because you have a soccer match, you won't be able to meet me at the train station when I arrive. So, give me directions from the train station to the soccer field.
  (response time = 30 seconds)
- After the soccer match we are both hungry. Suggest one of the restaurants for us to eat at. Give reasons why you think it would be a good place for us to eat.
  (response time = 30 seconds)
- Over dinner we talk. Tell me about a recent book you've read, and explain the reasons why you find it interesting.
  (response time = 60 seconds)

Practice Set 4 (refer to Map 2)

Imagine you are talking with your older sister, who is visiting from out of town.

- There is a large library in town. What are some reasons for going to a library?
  (response time = 30 seconds)
- I need to look at some newspapers at the library. Please tell me how to get from the post office to the library.
  (response time = 30 seconds)
- You just came from the library. Please tell me about your favorite newspaper or magazine and explain the reasons why you find it interesting.
  (response time = 60 seconds)

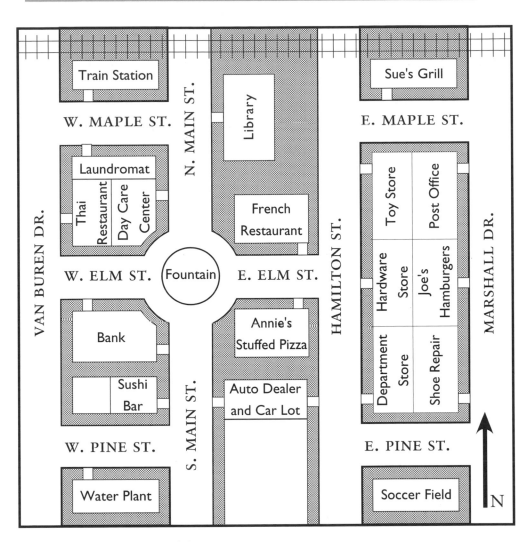

Map 2 for Practice Sets 3 and 4

Practice Set 5 (refer to Map 3)

Imagine that you work at this store and this is my first time to come here.

- I have been wanting to lose some weight and just started a diet. Suggest some food for me to buy. Justify your recommendations with reasons why you think these foods would be good for my diet? (response time = 30 seconds)
- I'm running late and need to pick up a few things quickly. I have just entered the store. Please give me directions from the apples to the toothpaste to the coffee. (response time = 30 seconds)
- This evening I have invited some friends over for a party. Please recommend some food I could serve. Justify your recommendation with reasons why you think this is good party food. (response time = 60 seconds)

Practice Set 6 (refer to Map 3)

Imagine that we are neighbors and run into each other at this store.

- I'm thirsty and am trying to pick out something to drink. Recommend one beverage. Justify your recommendation with reasons why you think I should buy it. (response time = 30 seconds)
- I'm not sure where to find a couple of items in the store. Please give me directions from the napkins to the sandwich meat to the carrots. (response time = 30 seconds)
- Please tell me about one of your favorite breakfast foods and explain the reasons why you like this food for breakfast. (response time = 60 seconds)

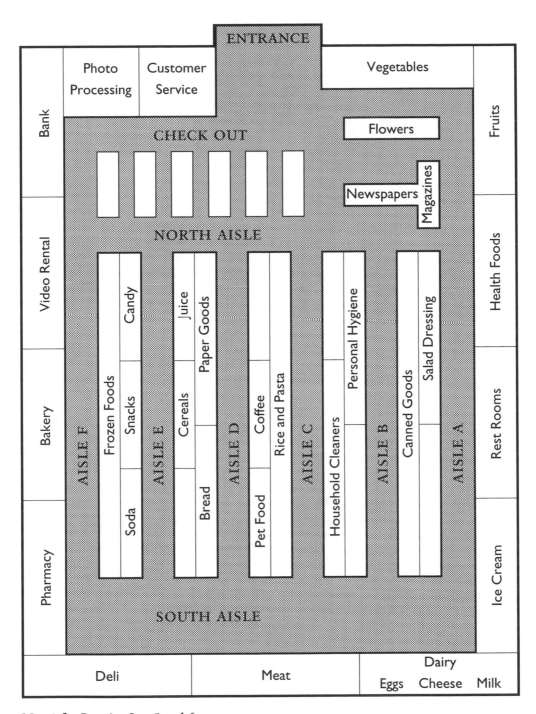

Map 3 for Practice Sets 5 and 6

Chapter 5
Picture Section

In this chapter you will:

- Become familiar with the instructions for questions 4, 5, 6, and 7 of the TSE;
- See examples of questions 4, 5, 6, and 7 and corresponding responses;
- Learn what makes an effective response to questions 4, 5, 6, and 7; and
- Practice responding to practice questions 4, 5, 6, and 7.

The general directions for the picture section of the test may be similar to this:

> **In this section of the test you will see six pictures that depict a story line. You will be given 60 seconds to review the pictures. After that you will be asked to tell the short story that is illustrated by the pictures. Try to include all six pictures in your story. When the test narrator tells you to, you may start telling the story.**

There are usually four questions that relate to the picture sequence immediately after the pictures. Use the 60 seconds to study the pictures wisely. During that time you should think of nouns, verbs, adjectives, and adverbs that are appropriate for the scene, people, and action depicted. Since the pronouns *he* and *she* can be potentially confusing, you may want to identify the characters with simple names like *Bob* and *Beth* or with descriptions like *the police officer* or *the bus driver*. The story usually will show some kind of conflict or problem, so take a few seconds to think of some way this problem could have been avoided. It can be helpful to imagine yourself as the main character and think about how you would react to the situation.

5a. Picture Section, Question 4

Question 4 may be similar to this:

> **Here are six pictures that illustrate a short story. Starting at the beginning, tell me the complete story picture by picture.**
> (response time = 60 seconds)

First of all you need to decide if you will tell the story in past or present tense. Whichever tense you choose, be sure you stick with it through the entire story. For some people it is helpful to take on the role of the main character in the story and to tell the story as if it were about yourself. Other people like to pretend they are seeing the story take place, and they describe what they see. You should decide which perspective you prefer. Don't spend too much time on any one picture. Your words should concentrate on the major idea shown in each picture. You can assume that the rater is looking at the pictures while listening to you. An example response to this question is:

> *It was a sunny day and John was walking through the park.*
> *Because it was hot John took off his sweater. The park had many*
> *beautiful trees and paths. In the park he saw where someone was*
> *renting bicycles. John liked bike riding and decided it would be*
> *nice to take a bike ride through the park. So he gave the cashier at*
> *the booth five dollars to rent a bike for one hour. At*
> *first John enjoyed his bike ride. He enjoyed the breeze in his face*
> *as he speeded along the bike path. In a short time John traveled a*
> *long way on his rented bike. Suddenly John hit a sharp rock with*
> *his front tire. The wheel went flat and John was no longer able to*
> *ride the bike. After John walked the bike back to the booth, he*
> *asked for his money back. The cashier told him that there were no*
> *refunds.*

This answer uses basic past tenses throughout the story such as *was, was walking, took off, had, saw, was renting, liked, decided, gave, enjoyed, speeded, traveled, hit, went, walked, asked, told,* and *were.* Since the story can be clearly communicated without using a variety of complex past tenses, it is easiest to stick with basic past tenses. The main character is given the name John. The other man is identified by his job of cashier. Notice that key action words are used to describe the pictures, like *walking, renting, enjoyed,* and *hit.* Key adjectives are used to describe only selected ideas suggested from the pictures, like *sunny day, beautiful trees,* and *sharp rock.* Insignificant details are not mentioned, such as the rock wall or the reflector on the bike tire. There is not enough time to talk about these minor details, and they would tend to distract the rater from understanding your primary message.

Cohesion is achieved through the use of expressions like *because* and *so.* *Because it was hot . . .* provides a transition from the weather in the scene to what the main character was wearing. *So he gave the cashier . . .* provides a transition from the statement that John likes bike riding to his actual renting of a bike. Cohesion can express new ideas, additional ideas, cause, effect, and contrast (Wennerstrom 1989). Cohesive devices are critical in making your ideas flow together in a logical order that communicates clearly to the rater.

1

2

3

4

5

6

Exercise 5.1

Now let's practice using cohesive words and expressions. Here are pairs of words. There are a number of ways to connect each pair. Write out at least three different ways. One example has been done for you.

1.   Tim . . . feel sick

     Tim . . . attend a party

     *   Although Tim feels sick, he still plans on attending the party.

     *   Because Tim was feeling sick, he decided not to attend the party.

     *   While attending the party, Tim started to feel sick.

2.   Briana . . . tired out

     Briana . . . take a vacation

     _____

     _____

     _____

3.   Julie . . . hungry

     Julie . . . go to a restaurant

     _____

     _____

     _____

4. Mark . . . research

   Mark . . . meet deadline

   _____

   _____

   _____

5. Connie . . . graduate

   Connie . . . look for a job

   _____

   _____

   _____

Here is an alternative response to this question that is more informal in tone and utilizes the first person pronoun *I*.

It was Saturday afternoon and I decided to take a walk through the park. It was the end of the spring term and I felt like I needed some fresh air and exercise. Pretty soon I saw a new bicycle rental place. I thought to myself, "It sure would be nice to go for a bike ride on such a beautiful day." So I paid the cashier and went for a ride. At first I enjoyed seeing the beautiful scenery while biking. Then suddenly I hit a sharp rock with the front tire of the bike. The wheel went flat immediately. I couldn't ride it and I had no way of fixing it. Sadly I pushed the bike all the way back to the rental place in the hot sun. What started out as a beautiful day ended in a frustrating experience.

5b. Picture Section, Question 5

Question 5 may be similar to this:

> **In order to avoid this problem, what specifically do you think could have been done?**
> (response time = 30 seconds)

In the initial 60 seconds you are given to study the picture story, you should anticipate this question by first identifying the main problem or conflict and then determining ways to avoid the problem. Listen to the question carefully. If the question is in conditional form, then the answer should be in conditional form. An *if-then* statement is a useful way to express the conditional form. Organize your answer by first clearly stating the problem, then offering one possible solution, and then concluding. Here is a sample response:

> *The biker needs to ride more carefully to avoid getting a flat tire. If the biker had watched the path instead of gazing at the trees and lake, then the biker could have steered the bike away from the sharp rock. It does not look like there are many rocks in the path, which means that this flat tire was just an unhappy coincidence. With a little care and a little luck this problem will probably not happen again soon.*

This response starts out with a clear statement of the problem and clues the rater that a simple solution will be discussed. Then the details of the solution are given. The *if-then* statement clearly explains the alternative solution and the result. The possible solution is *If the biker had watched the path instead of gazing at the trees and lake . . . .* The result from this solution is . . . *then the biker could have steered the bike away from the sharp rock.* Notice how details are used to clarify meaning. Instead of just saying *gazing away* the examinee responds with the details of *at the trees and lake.* Also, the appropriate tense is used in the *if-then* statement *had watched* and *could have steered away.* Again, transitions are important. The transition phrase *which means that* connects the ideas of *not many rocks* and *an unhappy coincidence.*

It is not necessary to give more than one alternative solution. If you try to say too much, you may rush yourself and hurt your communicative ability. Furthermore, if you try to say too much you may not have time to fully explain your ideas, thereby hurting your communicative ability. Try to speak for at least 75% of the time allotted.

The response above also includes a one sentence conclusion. Its conclusion emphasizes that the problem is easily avoided and leaves the rater with a clear understanding of what the examinee was trying to communicate. Hence the rater is left with a good impression of the communicative ability of this examinee.

With this type of question, avoid vague responses such as *This could have been avoided if he had been more careful.* This statement can apply to almost any accident or problem, so it is not very effective in communicating your ability to suggest specific solutions to problems. One technique to overcome vagueness is to imagine that your boss is asking you to suggest solutions. It would be unacceptable to simply suggest being more careful in answer to a problem your boss asked you to solve. Likewise it is unacceptable to give such a vague answer on the TSE. Here is another alternative response to this question:

The bike path needs to be maintained better in order to avoid flat tires. Workers should be hired to clear the path of rocks and branches on a regular basis. It would not take a lot of effort to make the path safe for bikers.

5c. Picture Section, Question 6

Question 6 may be similar to this:

> **Pretend that you are the bike rider portrayed in the pictures.
> After you have taken the bike back to the rental booth, you find
> out that the cashier will not return your money. You think you
> deserve a refund; however, the bike rental company has a policy
> of no refunds. After you arrive home you call the company's
> owner. Role play your telephone conversation to convince the
> owner to refund your five dollar rental fee.**
> (response time = 45 seconds)

This question asks you to imagine that this situation is happening to you. In order to role-play you must take on the feelings and goals of the character and express them in English. Since you are role-playing a phone call, the first thing you need to do is to greet the person on the other end of the phone and identify yourself. Be sure to speak in present tense because you are acting out the situation, not describing a past event. Typical phone greetings are *Hello* or *Hello. This is John Smith.* Since this is a one-sided phone conversation, you have to imagine that someone answers on the other end of the telephone. You will need to maintain the telephone call for 45 seconds without someone giving a response to your comments.

After the greeting, explain the reason you are calling, which in this case will include what happened and why you want your money back. Say the specific amount of money you expect to be refunded so the rater knows exactly what you hope to receive. In the United States most people will be polite but firm when making this type of request over the phone. The test task is asking you to use your language ability to persuade. Rude or overly commanding behavior generally is not considered very persuasive in the United States. Stating logical reasons for why you want your request granted will usually be more persuasive than demanding something be done.

Another facet of persuading is making some concessions in order to make it easier for the other person to do what you ask. In this situation you could offer to accept a $5.00 coupon for biking rather than demand the $5.00 cash back. Here is a sample response:

> *Hello. This is John Smith. Earlier today I rented a bicycle from your rental booth in the park and the bike I was riding had a flat tire. I then had to walk the bicycle back in the hot sun! This was exhausting and not much fun! You know, if you're going to be renting these bicycles, I think they should be in better condition. Furthermore, the bicycle paths need to be better maintained. There are rocks and litter all over the path; it is impossible not to hit something! So I would like to ask for my $5.00 back. . . . Well, if your policy doesn't allow refunds, at least you could give me a coupon for a free bicycle rental another day. . . . Thanks, I knew you'd understand.*

This answer starts with an appropriate telephone greeting. Since your identity as a test taker is supposed to remain unknown to the rater, do not use your real name in the greeting. Since the name John was arbitrarily chosen for question 4, it was used again here so as not to confuse the raters with a name change. The last name of Smith was arbitrarily chosen as well.

The speaker quickly identifies the reason for his call: *I rented a bicycle and . . . had a flat tire.* Descriptive words like *hot sun, exhausting,* and *not much fun* are used to explain why this was an inconvenience to the customer and encourage the owner to sympathize with the situation. To further persuade the owner, the speaker provides two reasons why the owner should take responsibility for the flat tire: the rental service needs to better maintain the bicycles and the bicycle paths. Along with logical organization, transitions and connections help to enhance the communicative power of the response. Expressions such as *Earlier today . . . , I then had to walk . . . , if you're going to . . . , Furthermore . . . , So I would like to . . . ,* and *Well, if . . .* help the response to flow smoothly.

The speaker is successful in expressing his request while remaining polite. The request is softened or made more polite by phrases like *I think . . .* and *I would like to ask . . . .* Exclamation points emphasize the need to speak persuasively and with passion in order to accomplish the desired goal. Additionally, U.S. speakers are frequent users of contractions in informal conversation, so a number of contractions are used, like *you're, doesn't,* and *you'd.* Contractions allow the speaker to sound fluent by maintaining the rhythm of English.

One important aspect of appropriateness of language is to call people by their names. Don't just put Miss, Ms., Mrs., or Mr. in front of someone's title, like Mr. Owner, Ms. Storekeeper, Miss Supervisor, or Mrs. Professor. These expressions are never used in real life. Role plays should sound realistic, so if necessary insert a name such as Mr. Johnson, Ms. Nelson, Miss Brown, or Professor Cole.

Brief pauses are indicated by the three dots (. . .) in the response. These pauses make for a more realistic role play and make the speaker sound more communicative. The last sentence concludes the phone conversation on a positive note. Since there is no one actually responding to you, you should assume that the owner is positively persuaded by your answer. The polite positive ending will leave the rater with a good impression of your ability to use English to persuade others.

Here is an alternative response to this question:

> *Hello. May I speak with the owner of the bike rental? . . . Thanks. Hello, Mr. Johnson? This is John Smith. I'd like to talk with you about a problem I had while renting one of your bikes in the park today. The bike I rented had a flat tire, so I had to walk the bicycle back to the rental booth in the hot sun! I spent $5.00 for a bike ride and spent most of the hour pushing the bike back! When I explained the situation to the cashier at the booth, he wasn't very helpful. This just doesn't seem fair to me! So, I would like to ask for my $5.00 back. . . . Yes, I can stop by this afternoon to pick it up. Thanks.*

Exercise 5.2

Here is a short list of polite expressions for making requests. See what others you can add to the list.

please
could you please
would you mind
if you don't mind
if it's not too much trouble
if it's not too much of an inconvenience

_____

_____

_____

_____

Exercise 5.3

Now choose a few of the expressions above to make a variety of requests. After each request suggested in the phrases below, write out a polite request. Then say your requests aloud.

1. borrow a book: _____

_____

_____

2. repeat that question: _____

_____

_____

3. set an appointment: _____

_____

_____

4. ask for the time: _____

_____

_____

5. ask a friend to proofread your paper: _____

_____

_____

6. ask for a ride home: _____

_____

_____

5d. Picture Section, Question 7

Question 7 may be similar to:

> **In the scene you see a person riding a bicycle. People have varying opinions about whether it is better to ride bicycles or drive cars. Pretend that you are talking to someone who has just arrived in the United States and tell them about the pros and cons of bicycles and cars as transportation.**
> (response time = 60 seconds)

This is the last question in section 3. The topic of the question will usually come from some idea presented in the pictures but will extend beyond what is shown in the pictures. Therefore, you have more freedom to use your own ideas in responding to this question. Take a few seconds to think and then begin your answer with a brief preview. Talk about two or three ideas; time does not allow for more. If the question specifically asks you to talk about two items, in this case bicycles and cars, then in your answer you should try to discuss both items. Be explicit in your discussion of advantages and disadvantages. While mentioning the advantages of one thing may imply a disadvantage for the other, don't expect raters to make this inference. After talking about both sides of the issue, briefly conclude your answer. Here is a sample response:

> *There are both advantages and disadvantages to getting around by either bicycle or car. Two important factors to consider when discussing transportation are cost and convenience. The advantages of owning a bicycle are that you can buy an inexpensive one for about $100 and the cost of maintenance is very low. On the other hand, a reliable car will cost thousands of dollars with hundreds of dollars spent each year on fuel, insurance, and regular maintenance. Convenience is another factor. It is not easy to travel long distances or in rainy weather on a bicycle, yet these pose no problem for a car. Furthermore, cars can carry more luggage than bikes. So if you have enough money, I recommend that you buy a car to use while you're in the U.S.*

Providing a preview of ideas to come adds cohesion to the whole response. The first two sentences provide the rater with a clear preview, that is, a discussion of the *advantages* and the *disadvantages* of both *bicycles* and *cars* as forms of transportation. The two specific features to be discussed, *cost* and *convenience,* are emphasized so the rater knows what to listen for.

Each sentence in the body of the response clearly identifies which type of vehicle is being discussed, either bicycles or cars, and which feature is being discussed, either cost or convenience. Details are given to support the statements that are made, like *you can buy* a bicycle *for about $100* and cars have ongoing expenses like *fuel, insurance, and regular maintenance.* Concrete examples rather than generalizations make your ideas communicate more readily to the rater. For example, instead of a general statement like, "It might be hard for a bicycle to get you somewhere," the response contained a specific example, *It is not easy to travel long distances or in rainy weather on a bicycle.*

Transitions throughout the response help to make the answer cohesive. The preview statement, *Two important factors . . . ,* was already identified as a cohesive device. *On the other hand, . . . Convenience is another factor, Furthermore, . . .* and *So if you have enough money . . .* are also examples of transitions.

The conclusion is short, just one sentence, but it summarizes the general intent of the response with a recommendation that demonstrates audience awareness by taking into account the listener's situation. This type of conclusion adds cohesion to the response and demonstrates control of the language.

Here is another possible alternative for responding to this question that is more informal in tone:

> *For living on campus, I think the advantages of owning a bike far outweigh the advantages of owning a car. For one thing, bikes are inexpensive. You can pick up a good bike for about a hundred bucks where a decent car will cost you a couple thousand. Second, there's a problem with parking. It's easy to find a bike rack at all the campus buildings to lock up your bike, but it's impossible to find a parking space for a car unless it's a weekend. You'll want to get a strong lock for your bike too, since every year lots of bikes are stolen. I know that during break you may want to do some traveling, and it would be nice to have a car for that. But don't worry, you can rent a car pretty cheaply, and if you travel with friends you can split the cost. While it may sound nice to own a car, I think you'll be better off getting around campus by bike.*

5e. Picture Section, Practice Questions

These practice questions will help you prepare to think quickly and respond concisely to picture section questions. You should study the sequence of six pictures shown with each practice set before answering the questions that follow. Work on one practice set at a time. If you preview all the questions at once, you will ruin the spontaneity. Make your practice as realistic as possible by not looking ahead at other questions and by keeping the time limit. For each set of questions below, tape-record your responses. Then listen to each response to see if you have accurately responded to the specific language function and if you have appropriately addressed the intended audience. Correct and repeat responses that need improvement.

Practice Set 1

- Here are six pictures that illustrate a short story. Starting at the beginning, tell me the complete story picture by picture.
  (response time = 60 seconds)
- In order to avoid this problem, what specific precautions could have been taken?
  (response time = 30 seconds)
- Pretend you are the customer who falls down in this scene. Role-play your discussion with the manager of this restaurant and convince her to replace your food free of charge.
  (response time = 45 seconds)
- A variety of foods are served at most restaurants. People have varying opinions about whether meat should be included in a person's diet. Pretend you are talking to a couple of your colleagues and tell them the pros and cons of both types of diets.
  (response time = 60 seconds)

Pictures for Practice Set 1

Practice Set 2

- Here are six pictures that illustrate a short story. Starting at the beginning, tell me the complete story picture by picture.
  (response time = 60 seconds)

- In order to avoid this problem, what specific precautions could have been taken?
  (response time = 30 seconds)

- Pretend that you are the person in this scene. You have an important date in about an hour and you want to make a good impression. You need to shower and change your clothes, but you can't leave with a dirty car. Role-play your discussion with your roommate and convince him or her to clean your car for you while you get yourself ready.
  (response time = 45 seconds)

- The person in this scene is shown with a car. People have varying opinions about purchasing and leasing cars. Pretend you are talking to a colleague and explain the pros and cons of purchasing versus leasing a car.
  (response time = 60 seconds)

Pictures for Practice Set 2

Practice Set 3

- Here are six pictures that illustrate a short story. Starting at the beginning, tell me the complete story picture by picture.
  (response time = 60 seconds)
- In order to avoid this problem, what specific precautions could have been taken?
  (response time = 30 seconds)
- Pretend that you are the person in this scene. Role-play your telephone conversation with your neighbor, the owner of the dog, and convince him to buy you new flowers.
  (response time = 45 seconds)
- In this scene there is a dog. People have varying opinions about pets. Pretend you are talking to a colleague and tell her about the pros and cons of owning a pet.
  (response time = 60 seconds)

1

2

3

4

5

6

Pictures for Practice Set 3

Practice Set 4

- Here are six pictures that illustrate a short story. Starting at the beginning, tell me the complete story picture by picture.
  (response time = 60 seconds)
- In order to avoid this problem, what specific precautions could have been taken?
  (response time = 30 seconds)
- Pretend you are a parent of a child with a new bicycle. The brakes on the bicycle break the first day your child uses it. You decide to take the bicycle back to the store. Role-play your discussion with the bicycle store manager and convince her to replace the broken parts free of charge.
  (response time = 45 seconds)
- Some families are large and others are small. Pretend that we are neighbors discussing the pros and cons of being the oldest child in a family and being the youngest child in a family.
  (response time = 60 seconds)

1

2

3

4

5

6

Pictures for Practice Set 4

Practice Set 5

- Here are six pictures that illustrate a short story. Starting at the beginning, tell me the complete story picture by picture.
  (response time = 60 seconds)
- Pretend the customer drops the new TV while carrying it from his car to his home. In order to avoid this problem, what specific precautions could have been taken?
  (response time = 30 seconds)
- Pretend you are the person in this scene. Although you already have a TV at home, you really want to buy this new one. Role-play your telephone conversation with your spouse and try to convince him or her that you should buy this new TV set.
  (response time = 45 seconds)
- Televisions have become common household items in the U.S. However, people have varying opinions about televisions. Pretend you are talking with a colleague and explain to her the pros and cons of having or not having a television set in your home.
  (response time = 60 seconds)

Pictures for Practice Set 5

Chapter 6
Graph Section

In this chapter you will:

- Become familiar with the instructions for questions 8, 9, 10, and 11 of the TSE;
- See examples of questions 8, 9, 10, and 11 and corresponding responses;
- Learn what makes an effective response to questions 8, 9, 10, and 11; and
- Practice responding to practice questions 8, 9, 10, and 11.

The general directions for the graph section may be similar to this:

The next few questions will ask you about your thoughts on a number of different issues. Feel free to think for a couple of seconds before you begin speaking. Try to answer as thoroughly as you can in the time given for each question.

The questions in this section cover a number of topics, and each question focuses on a different function of language. For example, question 8 may ask you to give and defend an opinion, and question 9 may ask you to define a term. In order to accomplish these communication goals in the small amount of time given to respond, you will need a strategy and some practice. The raters don't expect you to begin speaking immediately, so don't start speaking your response immediately after the question is given. Take a few seconds to organize your thoughts.

6a. Graph Section, Question 8

Question 8 may be similar to:

A number of large cities like Baltimore, Chicago, and Seattle have aquariums where people can view sea animals. However, people have varying opinions about whether sea animals should be taken out of nature and forced to live in small aquarium tanks. Please tell me your opinion about this question.
(response time = 60 seconds)

After the question is given, you should quickly decide on the opinion you will defend. It is not important for the purpose of the test which side of the issue you take; choose the side that is easiest for you to talk about and explain. Maybe in your heart you don't believe in aquariums, but it's hard for you to explain why you believe this in concrete, rational terms in English. If you know concrete reasons for keeping aquariums and it is easier for you to express these reasons in English, then go ahead and choose this side to defend. Here is a sample response:

I believe society should keep aquariums. Two important reasons for keeping aquariums are for research and public awareness. First of all, research done on sea animals at aquariums benefits sea animals in the wild. If humans are serious about helping sea animals live in the wild, we must do all we can to learn about sea animals through research both in the wild and in aquariums. Second, aquariums help to keep people interested in sea animals and aware of the growing number of endangered species. Children especially like aquariums, and if children grow up with a love for sea animals they will be more likely to make sacrifices to help make sure natural habitat is set aside for sea animals. So while some people think that aquariums are a bad place for individual sea animals to live, it's really the best way to help sea animal populations live better lives in our world.

The language function of this question is to give and defend an opinion. In this response the opinion is given at the beginning and clearly accomplishes the function of giving an opinion. That is a good way to begin since it lets the rater know exactly what side is being defended. The second sentence gives a clear preview of the two main ideas to be discussed, *research* and *public awareness.*

The language function of defending an opinion is accomplished in the body of the response. In defending an opinion it is important to consider the arguments of the other side. Someone opposed to aquariums is likely to say that aquariums take away freedom from sea animals and sea animals may be unhappy or unhealthy in aquariums. To counter the opposing arguments, the response shows that sea animals in aquariums help sea animals in the wild through the knowledge gained through research and the support gained by public awareness.

Cohesion is maintained with a transition to the body of the answer: *First of all* . . . . The next main idea is also introduced with a transition: *Second,* . . . . The last sentence provides a summary of the answer: more sea animals are helped by keeping a few of them in aquariums. A clear summary leaves the rater with a strong impression that this response has accomplished the language functions of giving and defending an opinion.

Another possible response that supports the opposite view in a coherent manner is given on page 75.

Aquariums are definitely degrading to ocean animals. Both the size of the tanks and their forced dependence on humans show disrespect for these majestic forms of wildlife.

Living space is of primary concern. Take whales for example; no matter how big you build the tank, it will never be deep enough or wide enough to give the whale the freedom it deserves.

Second is the forced dependence on humans that ocean animals experience when held in captivity. The shark is a good example. Sharks were designed as hunters; when they are forced to give up hunting, as they are in aquariums, they lose their natural identities.

Although aquariums are popular, I never visit them because it breaks my heart to see these wonderful ocean animals in small tanks and forced to eat at the bidding of their keepers.

Exercise 6.1

Now take some time to practice thinking of reasons quickly. Under each of the five statements below, list at least three reasons. Allow a total of five minutes to list reasons for all five statements. Time yourself.

1. Commuters in urban areas should be required to carpool.

   _____

   _____

   _____

2. A college education should be mandatory.

   _____

   _____

   _____

3. A course in ethics should be required for all college degrees.

    _____

    _____

    _____

4. Doctors should deliver babies in the mother's home.

    _____

    _____

    _____

5. The federal government should provide a free computer to every home.

    _____

    _____

    _____

Now choose one of the topics above and with a partner or on a tape recorder present the given argument with the reasons you have listed. Evaluate the organization of your reasons, the transitions between reasons, and the opening and closing of your argument.

6b. Graph Section, Question 9

Question 9 may be similar to:

> **Pretend you are a graduate student and a group of high school students come to visit your campus. As you give them a tour of your department define and explain a basic concept in your area of study.**
> (response time = 60 seconds)

Defining a concept or term is a language function you should think about and prepare for. The test may provide something specific to define or may give you the freedom to pick a concept or term of your choice within a given range of possibilities, as in the sample question above. Generally, it is not useful to memorize definitions, because it is too difficult to predict what you might be asked for on the test. Additionally, memorized responses tend to focus the speaker on remembering the "right words" rather than on communicating the message to a specific audience with the appropriate intonation and rhythm. Furthermore, memorizing definitions may tempt the speaker to give a memorized definition as an answer to a question although the term itself or the phrasing may not fit the given audience and context. Raters can generally identify memorized answers and rate them down accordingly. Nonetheless, it will help you to have practiced defining concepts and terms ahead of time so you will develop a strategy for defining any concept or term asked of you. The strategy for defining a term outlined below is adapted from Smith, Meyers, and Burkhalter (1992).

1. Clearly state the concept or term you are defining.
2. Explain the importance of this concept or term.
3. Give a concise definition of the concept or term.
4. Provide examples or analogies that relate to your listeners and help clarify the concept or term.
5. Conclude your definition by emphasizing key ideas or by motivating your listeners.

With practice you can learn to apply this strategy for defining concepts and terms in order to maximize the effectiveness of your communication.

The first thing to do in responding to a definition question is to choose a concept. You should select something that is very simple because you only have one minute to define it. Since the question implies that the audience has no background in your field, try to pick a concept that most people have heard of before. In this way, as you speak the rater may recall what he or she already knows about this concept. If you choose an obscure term, then the rater may be unable to relate anything you say to his or her own knowledge or experience. Picking somewhat familiar terms or concepts is important because your communicative ability will be rated, in part, by how well you respond to a particular audience.

Here is a sample response:

> *The concept I would like to define for you is concrete. Concrete is a very important substance because it is a basic material for most construction projects like large buildings and airports. Concrete is composed of 3 parts, aggregate, cement, and water. Aggregate includes gravel and sand. Cement acts as a glue. Water is necessary to start the binding action of the cement. One way to understand concrete is to think of the candy called peanut brittle. Peanuts can be compared to aggregate. Sugar and water are mixed to form a syrup that dries to hold the peanuts in peanut brittle. This is similar to the way cement and water dry to hold the aggregate in concrete. Sometimes peanut brittle gets pretty hard, but concrete is even harder. That is why concrete is an excellent material for construction.*

The concept chosen for this response was *concrete.* This is a good choice because most people have a general idea of what concrete is and how it is used, though they may not know its composition. The response begins with a clear statement that the concept to be discussed is *concrete.* It is important that the rater knows what you are defining before you go into the details of a definition. It is also important to tell why the concept is important. The second sentence of the response says that concrete is important . . . *because it is a basic material for most construction projects . . .* and then goes on to give specific examples of projects . . . *like large buildings and airports.* Specific examples help the rater to better understand the ideas expressed.

Next a formal definition of concrete is given. In this case concrete is formally defined by the parts that go together to make it, *aggregate, cement, and water.* Cohesion is maintained by defining each of the three parts in the order it was mentioned. Long chemical names are avoided because they may be difficult to pronounce and the rater may not understand even if they are pronounced correctly. Formulas and other technical details are avoided because there is only a short time to respond, and these would more than likely confuse the rater and detract from communication.

After the formal definition, an analogy is given to help a nonexpert understand a technical term. This may be the hardest part of the strategy for giving a definition. Generally it takes people time to think of and develop analogies. So if an analogy does not readily come to mind, this may be something that is skipped in your definition. However, analogies are a powerful way for you to communicate to nonexperts the basic ideas of your technical term. In this response the analogy is introduced with a transition: *One way to understand concrete* . . . . Choose an analogy that most people are familiar with. *Peanut brittle* was chosen in this case. This is a candy most people know about. Avoid analogies with complex items because they cause you to focus on explaining the analogy rather than the concept, and in the end communication suffers. When using analogies, make clear connections to your concept. In this response *peanuts* were compared with *aggregate,* and *sugar and water* were compared with *cement and water.* Specific expressions are used to make this relationship clear, like *compared to* and *similar to.* The analogy even extends to the strength of the material: . . . *peanut brittle gets pretty hard, but concrete is even harder.*

If an analogy does not readily come to mind, you should try to include examples that help to make your term more relevant to your audience. If the peanut brittle analogy were not used in this response, there are other examples that could have been shared instead. It is possible to give examples of how the strength of concrete is put to use, as shown in the alternative response below.

The last two sentences bring closure to the response and keep it cohesive. First of all the conclusion emphasizes that concrete is *hard* and second that concrete is an *excellent material for construction.* This response follows the five-step strategy for defining concepts or terms presented earlier. This is a solid strategy for communicating the definition and explanation of a concept or term. If you use this strategy well, you communicate a sense of fluency, knowledge, and confidence to the rater.

Here is an alternative response that focuses on examples rather than on an analogy:

> *When we walk through the engineering lab, you'll have a chance to see some of the student projects involving concrete. While you all may know what concrete looks like, you may not know what it's made of. Concrete has three basic components, aggregate, cement, and water. Aggregate includes gravel and sand. Cement acts as a glue. Water is necessary to start the binding action of the cement. Concrete has many uses in society. Concrete foundations hold the weight of large buildings. Concrete runways endure the repeated landings of jumbo jets. Concrete dams hold back tons of water. Concrete can also make our lives more pleasant in smaller ways, like concrete sidewalks for our neighborhoods and concrete benches for our parks. Anyway, concrete is not something that's taken for granted by our engineering faculty and students.*

Exercise 6.2

Now let's work on quickly thinking of examples, because specific examples can be an effective method for communicating ideas. For each of the categories below, list two or three examples. Make sure your examples are specific and relevant to the topic.

1. How to lose weight

_____

_____

_____

2. The benefits of having someone else proofread a paper you write

_____

_____

_____

3. The costs and benefits of a state lottery

    _____

    _____

    _____

4. The importance of voting in a democracy

    _____

    _____

    _____

5. Surfing the World Wide Web

    _____

    _____

    _____

Now choose one of the topics, *losing weight, proofreading, lottery, democracy,* or *World Wide Web.* Define it orally and include the examples from your list.

6c. Graph Section, Question 10

One or two test questions usually relate to a graph given in the test. When there are two questions about the graph, the first question will usually ask you to perform the language function of describing a graph. Question 10 may be similar to:

> **The ability to read and write is considered an important factor for nations. Here is a graph for one specific nation that shows the percentages of this nation's population that are able to read and write. I am also looking at this graph, but I need you to tell me about the data portrayed in it.**
>
> (response time = 60 seconds)

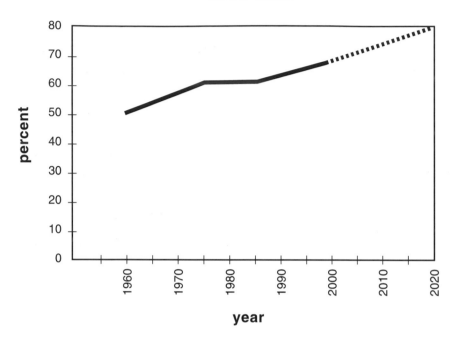

Take a few seconds to review the graph before you start speaking. Although you don't know what graph you will be asked to describe until you see it on the test, you should have a strategy for describing graphs before the test. Smith, Meyers, and Burkhalter (1992) provide some excellent tips for describing visuals like a graph. This strategy is summarized below.

1. Introduce the graph by giving its title or purpose.
2. Discuss the overall organization of the graph.
3. Explain any symbols, terms, or other information that may be new for your audience.
4. Give at least one specific example that demonstrates the information provided in the graph.
5. Discuss overall trends, patterns, or predictions based on the graph.
6. Close by summarizing the points you want to emphasize about the graph.

[handwritten note: esoteric ← correct spelling]

[handwritten note: Nonetheless]

[handwritten note: None the less ← correct pronunciation]

[handwritten note: esoteric]

Wi_____ _____ for describing graphs in
ord_____ _____ unication. Here is a
sam_____

_____ om 1960 to 2020.
_____ ut 1960 and going to
_____ of this nation's
_____ the literacy rate of
_____ or example, in 1960
_____ erate. The solid line
sh___ _____ for positive growth in the literacy rate of this
nation's population over the past 35 years. The dashed line shows
a projected increase in the literacy rate to about 80% by the year
2020. So, from this graph we learn that the literacy rate of this
nation's population has steadily increased over the past 35 years
and is projected to further increase into the Twenty-first Century.

A good way to start your response is to state the title of the graph. Stating
the title helps you get started with your answer, and a simple expression like
The title of this graph is . . . sounds fluent and clearly tells the rater what you
will be describing. If the graph includes years, don't just read the numbers
like *1960, 2020.* Instead, package them in prepositions and say *from 1960 to
2020.* This creates fluency rather than a halting reading of what's written on
the page. The easiest way to pronounce years before the year 2000 is to
break them in half; so rather than saying *one thousand nine hundred and fifty,*
the year can be stated simply as *nineteen fifty.* On the other hand, years
coming after 2000 can be read as *two thousand* plus the additional year. So
2020 can be stated as *two thousand twenty.*

The response goes on to explain both the horizontal and vertical axes
with the straightforward expressions *The horizontal axis shows . . .* and *The
vertical axis shows . . . .* Since most graphs include axes, you should learn to
pronounce these terms correctly. When contrasting the definitions of the

two axes, the primary stress should be placed on the underlined part as follows: horizontal axis and vertical axis. The same contrasting stress pattern applies if you are describing the x-axis and the y-axis. Also note that the vowel quality of the word *axis* changes between the singular and plural forms. The singular form, axis, is pronounced with a short /i/ sound as in fit, and the plural form, axes, is pronounced with a long /e/ sound as in feet.

A transition sentence is used to move from a description of the axes to reading a particular point on the graph: *For any given year the literacy rate of this nation's population can be determined.* To highlight the specific example, the phrase *For example, . . .* is used. Other useful phrases for marking your examples are *for instance . . . , to show what I mean . . . , to illustrate that . . . , a case in point . . . .* Do not waste a lot of time trying to read information off the graph to the nearest hundredth. Choose what looks like a reasonable number for a specific point on the graph and use a word like *approximate* or *about* to qualify your answer. This is an acceptable approach when reading a graph that does not show much detail.

Next the symbols on the graph are identified; in this case two different line types are used. Each line type is clearly identified; *The solid line shows . . .* and *The dashed line shows . . . .* Other useful descriptions of lines include *dotted line, straight line, curved line, horizontal line,* and *vertical line.* Some graphs contain shaded areas that might need to be explained. These can be identified with expressions such as *the shaded area, the dotted area, the blackened area,* and *the cross-hatched area* (Smith, Meyers, and Burkhalter 1992).

Because graphs usually contain a lot of information, it is useful to talk about trends, patterns, or predictions that graphs show. In this response the trend for an increase in the literacy rate was noted with the phrase *a trend for positive growth.* A time frame for this trend is also identified: *. . . over the past 35 years.* Although the rate of growth in the literacy rate changed at about 1975, the trend gives a general description, not a specific year by year or decade by decade analysis. Since there is not a lot of time given to respond, smaller details like the changes in the rate of population growth in 1975 are not included. Words and phrases that are useful to describe trends and patterns include *increase, decrease, rise, fall, decline, drop, jump, leveling* *off,* and *plateau.* Adjectives that can be used to describe change include *rapid, slow, sudden, gradual, moderate, exponential,* and *consistent.*

Including a summary statement at the end of an answer allows you to bring closure to your discussion and demonstrates fluency and control of language. In the response above, the summary statement is marked with the transition *So . . . .* This concluding statement summarizes the main trend of the graph *. . . the literacy rate of this nation's population has steadily increased over the past 35 years . . .* and also makes a prediction about the future *. . . is projected to further increase into the Twenty-first Century.* When the response is finished, the rater has a good idea of what the graph is about and has a positive impression of the language used to communicate that description.

Here is an alternative response that explains the graph. This response is organized from left to right.

> *As we study the development of various nations, one important factor to consider is literacy. The national literacy rate of one particular country we would like to study is shown in this graph. The horizontal axis shows literacy data from 1960 to the present, as well as projected data up to the year 2020. The vertical axis shows the literacy rate in percentages. In 1960 the literacy rate was approximately 50%, with a gradual increase until 1975. From 1975 to 1985 the literacy rate stagnated at around 60%. From 1985 to the present the literacy rate has been on a gradual rise. The dashed portion of the line shows the future literacy rate projected at 80% by the year 2020. So except for a brief period, the literacy rate in this nation has been increasing over the last 35 years and is projected to increase through 2020.*

Exercise 6.3

Now let's practice explaining a graph that you create yourself. The axes and the line of an imaginary graph are shown below. Think of something this graph might describe. Fill in the horizontal axis with numbers representing days, years, temperature, weight, cost, or whatever. Next fill in the vertical axis with number of people, number of sales, pressure, cost, or whatever. Be sure to label each of the axes. Next write in a title for your graph. Now describe your graph to a partner or tape-record yourself and listen. Using the six point strategy, assess how well you have communicated the information in your graph.

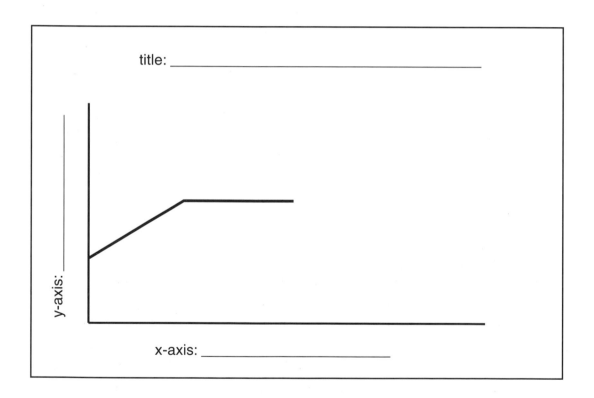

title: _____

y-axis: _____

x-axis: _____

Exercise 6.4

Find a graph in a newspaper, magazine, or book. Many newspapers like *USA Today* and the *Wall Street Journal* are good sources for graphs. Record yourself describing the graph for one minute. Using the six point strategy, assess how well you communicated the information in the graph.

6d. Graph Section, Question 11

Often there is an additional question that follows the question about describing a graph. Rather than focusing on the graph itself, this question extends beyond it. You may be asked to perform the language function of discussing, such as discussing what the graph implies about the future. Question 11 may be similar to:

Although the future is uncertain, please discuss how you think literacy could affect the future of this particular nation.
(response time = 45 seconds)

This response can begin where the last response ended since the conclusion of the description of the graph mentioned the projected increase in the literacy rate. A good way to begin the response to this question is to clearly state what the graph predicts. However, this is not the main function of this question. The main language function is to discuss. So you should not merely describe what the graph is predicting but should discuss what effect it may have on the future. Here is a sample response:

This graph predicts that the literacy rate of this nation will continue to increase between now and the year 2020. This means that more people in this country will have the opportunity to both read about other people's ideas and to write down their own ideas for others to read. For example, a literate person may have access to libraries and all the written information available on the World Wide Web. Written information from literature to science can be intellectually stimulating for a literate individual. Likewise, a literate person can write down his or her own ideas and feelings for others to read. Literate people can communicate through letters, e-mail, or books. So increasing the literacy rate of this nation helps to build a nation of individuals that can exchange ideas and feelings through reading and writing.

This response starts with a clear statement of what the graph says about the future. The word *predicts* is a concise way to talk about what is expected to happen in the future. *Increase* clearly states what change is expected. Less important details, such as *the percentage will increase from 50% to 80% by the year 2020,* are avoided in order to respond effectively within the time allotted. Notice that the sentence clearly identifies what the graph describes, *the literacy rate of this nation.* This is the *literacy rate or percentage* of that nation's population, not the *total number of people.* If your wording does not accurately describe what the graph shows, then the rater may doubt your ability to accurately communicate specific information. The opening sentence also identifies the time frame of this prediction: *between now and the year 2020.*

Next, two specific benefits based on the graph's predictions are presented: *the opportunity to both read about other people's ideas and to write down their own ideas for others to read.* This acts as a preview and clues the rater to listen for more about the benefits of reading and the benefits of writing. The 45 second response time is even shorter than that given for the last two questions, so it is essential to be brief and to the point. If you try to talk about more than two points, you may not have time to finish explaining your ideas and your communication may be hindered, which in turn may reduce how well the raters understand you.

This response communicates to the rater why reading and writing benefit an individual. The response connects the *opportunity to read* with *other people's ideas* and the *opportunity to write* with sharing *ideas for others to read.* To clarify these ideas specific examples are given both for reading and for writing. The example for reading refers to *access to libraries* and *the World Wide Web.* The example for writing refers to *letters, e-mail,* and *books.* The use of specific examples that support your ideas communicates to the raters that you are able to use language to clearly express your ideas.

The conclusion is marked with the transition *So . . . .* In the conclusion the main points are summarized: *exchange ideas and feelings through reading and writing.* Appropriate pausing can be used in this concluding sentence to emphasize the key ideas. The slashes (/) marked below show where pausing can be used effectively in the concluding sentence. *So/ increasing the literacy rate/ of this nation/ helps to build a nation of individuals/ that can exchange ideas and feelings/ through reading and writing./* With clauses that begin with *that,* it is generally more effective to pause before *that* rather than after. Some speakers might pause before the two *ands;* however, in this case the phrases *ideas and feelings* and *reading and writing* are more closely connected by not pausing at the *ands.* By using appropriate pausing, you convey your meaning more easily, and the rater is left with a good impression of your communicative ability.

Here is an alternative response that focuses on the relationship of literacy to the economy:

> *Literacy is a key factor for this nation to grow and prosper in today's world. A successful national economy depends both on technology and international trade. Business and manufacturing are depending more and more on computers and hi-tech equipment, and these take literate people to design and operate them. Besides, national economies are no longer isolated from the world. A literate workforce is essential for this nation to be involved in importing and exporting. Therefore, a growing literacy rate should have positive effects on this nation's economy.*

6e. Graph Section, Practice Questions

These practice questions will help you prepare to think quickly and respond concisely to the types of questions found in the graph section. Work on one practice set at a time. If you preview all the questions at once, you will ruin the spontaneity. Make your practice as realistic as possible by not looking ahead at other questions and by keeping the time limit. For each set of practice questions below, tape-record your responses. As you listen to your recorded responses, see if you have accurately responded to the specific language function and if you have appropriately addressed the intended audience. Correct and repeat responses that need improvement.

Practice Set 1

- People have varying opinions about whether it is better to live in large urban areas or rural areas. Please tell me your opinion about this question.
  (response time = 60 seconds)
- Although we are friends, we are interested in different career areas. Think about a typical job position in your field and define and explain for me about the responsibilities of someone with this position.
  (response time = 60 seconds)
- A college education is valued by many people. Here is a graph for one specific state that shows the percentage of this state's population that has received college degrees. I am also looking at this graph, but I need you to tell me about the data portrayed in it.
  (response time = 60 seconds)

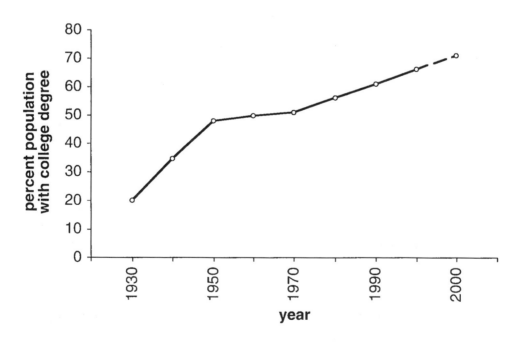

**College Degrees
in a Specific State**

- Please discuss how you think the amount of college degrees granted could affect the future of this particular state.
  (response time = 45 seconds)

Practice Set 2

- Due to budget cuts, some schools have to cut some of their programs. People have varying opinions about whether art courses, band, and orchestra should be eliminated or whether physical education and sports teams should be cut. What is your opinion? Which programs do you think schools should cut and why?
  (response time = 60 seconds)

- Pretend that I am a friend who is not familiar with the equipment used in your profession. Think about one tool, piece of equipment, or machinery used frequently in your field and define and explain for me how it is used.
  (response time = 60 seconds)

- Part of the American Dream is owning your own home. Here is a graph for one specific region that shows information on new home construction. I am also looking at this graph, but I need you to tell me about the data portrayed in it.
  (response time = 60 seconds)

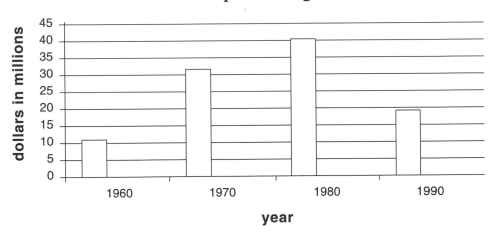

New Home Construction in a Specific Region

- Please discuss why owning your own home is such an important part of the American Dream.
  (response time = 45 seconds)

Practice Set 3

- It has been suggested that the United States should not use pennies for currency anymore, yet not everyone agrees. Please tell me your opinion about this question.
  (response time = 60 seconds)
- Pretend that I am a student in your class. Define and explain for me what you mean by plagiarism.
  (response time = 60 seconds)
- Illustrated here is a graph that shows the number of televisions in different counties of a state. I am also looking at this graph, but I need you to tell me about the data portrayed in it.
  (response time = 60 seconds)

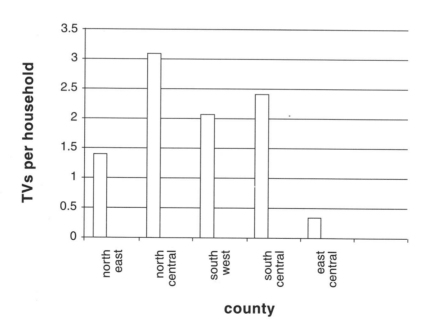

Televisions within Counties

- Please discuss how you think the distribution of televisions could affect the future of the people in these different counties.
  (response time = 45 seconds)

Practice Set 4

- Health care is an issue that affects everyone. Should the national government provide health care for all citizens or should citizens be responsible for their own health care? Please tell me your opinion about this question.
  (response time = 60 seconds)
- Pretend that I'm a friend who is not familiar with your field of study. Please define and explain for me the type of research that is considered excellent in your field.
  (response time = 60 seconds)
- Illustrated here is a graph that shows the sales of fax machines and car phones for a specific region. I am also looking at this graph, but I need you to tell me about the data portrayed in it.
  (response time – 60 seconds)

Car Phone & Fax Sales

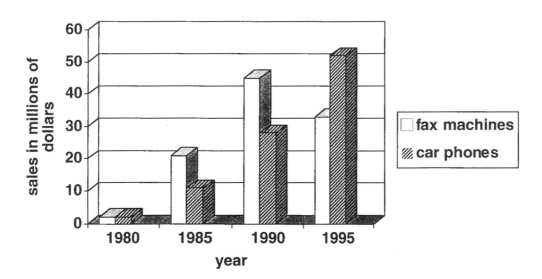

- Please discuss how you think faxes and car phones have affected communication in this region.
  (response time = 45 seconds)

Practice Set 5

- Through modern technology, parents can be informed of the gender of their baby before it is born. Yet people have varying opinions about whether a baby's gender should be disclosed before birth or not. Please tell me your opinion about this question.
  (response time = 60 seconds)

- Pretend that you are at a party where no one else attending the party has been to your country. Your friends at the party are interested in the government of your country. Choose one branch or division of government of your country and define and explain it for your friends.
  (response time = 60 seconds)

- Illustrated here is a graph that shows the sales for computers in a specific region. I am also looking at this graph, but I need you to tell me about the data portrayed in it.
  (response time = 60 seconds)

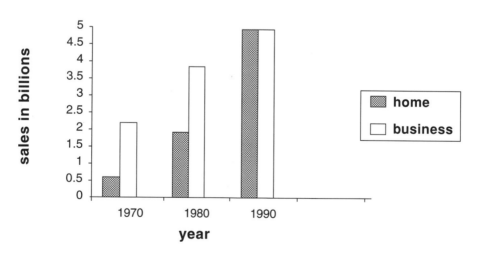

Computer Sales

- Please discuss how you think computer sales could affect the future of the people in this region.
  (response time = 45 seconds)

Chapter 7

Announcement Section

In this chapter you will:

- Become familiar with the instructions for question 12 of the TSE;
- See examples of question 12 and corresponding responses;
- Learn what makes an effective response to question 12; and
- Practice responding to practice question 12.

7a. Announcement Section, Question 12

This is the final question of the exam. You are asked to role-play the part of someone giving an announcement. The announcement will usually have some changes marked on it, and these are the details you should highlight in your announcement. Also think about the intended audience and what is the best way to address this specific group. Question 12 may be something like the question on page 96.

Let's pretend that you are the president of the Glenview Historical Society. On this page you will see an agenda for a trip to Springfield, Illinois. As president of the Glenview Historical Society you have had the responsibility for planning this trip. You mailed a copy of the trip agenda to all the Glenview Historical Society members two weeks ago. Since then, you noticed some errors and some last minute revisions. Pretend you are at the monthly meeting of the Glenview Historical Society and you want to review the schedule of the trip with the other members and emphasize the corrections in the agenda. Because this is an oral presentation to the members of your organization you do not want to simply read the information printed on the agenda. Take the next 60 seconds to think about your presentation. On the actual test you will hear the test narrator ask you to begin your presentation.
(response time = 90 seconds)

In responding to this type of question it is important to role-play the part, that is, imagine that you really are the president of the organization and that you really are talking to the members. It is important to choose language that is appropriate for your audience and for the task of expressing the details of the schedule and highlighting the scheduling changes. Reading the information from the printed schedule word for word or without organizational markers or transitions will result in an artificial telegraphic sound and a lower score.

You are given 60 seconds to review the schedule before you need to start speaking. Since you have been asked not to read the information, think of language you can use to package the information in a way that is appropriate to the context. Practice pronouncing words you think you may have trouble saying clearly. For example, if you have trouble pronouncing /th/ or /r/, then consciously practice pronouncing *Thursday* and *thirteen*. Additionally, prepare an opening statement to greet the audience and tell them what you will be talking about. As you look over the details of the schedule, think of ways you can highlight the changes. Also think of a way to bring your presentation to a close. Look at page 98 for a sample response.

GLENVIEW HISTORICAL SOCIETY
Springfield Trip

Date: ~~Thursday~~ Friday, October 13

Transportation: Glenview Club Van

Departure: ~~8:00~~ 7:30 a.m.   Jefferson Community College

Agenda: 10:00 a.m.   Guided tour of Lincoln's home
                12:00 p.m.   Memorial Carillon (special demonstration)
                12:30 p.m.   Lunch at Washington Park Botanical Gardens*
                2:00 p.m.   The Lincoln Tomb, Oakridge Cemetery
                3:00 p.m.   Illinois State ~~Museum~~ Capitol

Return: 5:00 p.m.

Cost: $~~5.00~~ 3.00 per person (to help cover gas)

---

*Bring your own lunch; drinks available for purchase at the park.

Good afternoon, ladies and gentlemen of the Glenview Historical Society. You are all invited on our trip to Springfield. Let's take a few minutes to review the schedule together. Our trip will take place on Friday, October 13th, not Thursday as was misprinted in the schedule. We will be taking the van, which is very comfortable, and will be leaving from Jefferson Community College at 7:30 a.m. Don't come at 8:00 as originally scheduled or you will miss the van!

Four activities are planned for our time in Springfield. At 10:00 a.m. we will start with a tour of Lincoln's home. From there we will drive to Memorial Carillon for a special noontime demonstration of the bells. This will be followed by lunch at 12:30 p.m. at the Washington Park Botanical Gardens. You should plan on bringing your own lunch, although drinks can be purchased there. At 2:00 p.m. our sight-seeing continues at the Lincoln Tomb. Because the Illinois State Museum is closed this week for repairs, we will be touring the Illinois State Capitol instead. Our van will be leaving from the capitol at approximately 5:00 p.m.

The cost of the trip is $3, not $5 as originally estimated. If you haven't signed up already, be sure to sign up today before you leave!

This response begins with a formal greeting from the president of a society to its members: *Good afternoon, ladies and gentlemen* . . . . A teaching assistant addressing a class or a student addressing other students who are part of a campus club would probably start out with a less formal greeting like *Hello everyone.* However, a professor presenting a paper at a conference or an executive giving a report to the board of directors would probably use a formal type of greeting. Therefore, it is important that you know what role you are supposed to be playing and what audience you are supposed to be talking to in order to appropriately address the audience.

The greeting is followed by a preview of what is to be shared in the announcement. The topic of the trip is introduced with an invitation *You are all invited . . . .* Then the preview specifically states, *Let's take a few minutes to review the schedule together.* This type of preview tells the audience and the rater what to listen for in the next few minutes. Because the rater provides clues on how to listen, the communication is more effective.

Public speakers as well as teachers often use inclusive language in order to show unity with the group they are speaking to. Therefore, rather than saying *I will tell you . . . ,* the phrase *Let's take a few minutes . . .* was used. Identifying the trip as *our trip* rather than *the trip* and stating that *We will be taking the van . . .* rather than *the van will be leaving . . .* makes the announcement sound more inclusive as well. Expressions like *our time in Springfield . . . , we will start with . . . , our sight-seeing continues . . . , we will be touring . . . ,* and *our van will be leaving . . .* all add to the inclusiveness of the announcement, which is the type of atmosphere a president would want to create in his or her organization.

Exercise 7.1

Dates, places, and times should be accurately stated to avoid confusion. Except for *first, second,* and *third,* dates carry a voiceless /th/ sound as in *April twelfth.* Most announcements include some kind of dates. Before you take the test, practice pronouncing the twelve months of the year along with various dates such as:

January first	February twelfth	March thirteenth
April fourteenth	May fifteenth	June sixteenth
July seventeenth	August eighteenth	September nineteenth
October twenty-fifth	November thirtieth	December thirty-first

During the 60 seconds given to prepare your announcement, check your pronunciation of key words including all multisyllable place names and nouns. In this example that would include *Glenview Historical Society, Springfield, Illinois, Jefferson Community College, Memorial Carillon, Washington Park Botanical Gardens, Lincoln Tomb, Oak Ridge Cemetery, Illinois State Museum,* and *Illinois State Capitol.*

Times can be clearly stated by referring to either a.m. or p.m. In this response, the first morning time was given as 7:30 a.m. When 8:00 was mentioned right after this, no a.m. was used since the time frame had already been established as morning. Clear communication of dates, places, and times allows the rater to accurately follow your announcement, which can strengthen your communicative ability.

The schedule of the trip is given in a logical order starting with the date and the departure time and going through each of the activities in order. This is the way the information was presented on the written announcement. Talking about the details of the schedule in this order makes it easier for the raters to follow your announcement as they follow along on their own copy of the schedule.

Since the schedule will probably have some changes marked on it, you will need to think of wording that can highlight these changes. To make changes clear, the new information is given along with the old information so the audience doesn't just assume that the printed schedule is correct and not note down the changes. For example, if all that was announced was Friday, October 13th, then a listener might not realize that the 13th was a Friday, not a Thursday. This type of confusion is avoided in the response with the phrase *Friday, October 13th, not Thursday as was misprinted in the schedule*. This contrast of old and new information should further be highlighted by placing primary phrase stress on *Friday* and *Thursday*. The change in plans for the departure time is highlighted in a similar way: *Don't come at 8:00 as originally scheduled or you will miss the van*. The cost of the trip was also changed and the change pointed out: *The cost of the trip is $3, not $5 as originally estimated*. To highlight this contrast primary phrase stress should be placed on *$3* and *$5*. (For more practice with primary phrase stress on contrasts see Dickerson and Hahn 1998).

When announcements contain both old information and new information, it is important to clearly state which is right and which is wrong. Clear statements are made in this response about what is incorrect information: *. . . not Thursday as was misprinted, Don't come . . . , . . . touring the Illinois State Capitol instead . . .* , and *. . . not $5*. Clear distinctions between old information and correct information will help to increase your communicative competence rating.

Often there will be an asterisk within the schedule that refers to a footnote at the bottom of the page. Include the footnoted information where appropriate and use complete sentences to explain the footnote. Choose language that relates the information in the footnote to the context of the announcement. Don't just tack on the footnote as an incomplete phrase at the end of your announcement.

As the person giving the announcement, you want to arouse the audience's interest in the information by making it interesting and relevant to them. However, there is not a lot of time to say much beyond what is in the written announcement. Adjectives can be used to create interest with expressions such as *. . . the van, which is very comfortable,* and *. . . special noontime demonstration*. However, be careful not to get sidetracked from the basic announcement. Notice how this response does not try to capture the interest of the audience by discussing the beauty of Washington Park or the details of the Memorial Carillon demonstration. If you try to make the announcement more interesting by adding a lot of details that are not in the written announcement, then you will not have time to fully explain the changes in the announcement as the question asks. This will leave the rater with the sense that the stated goal of telling the basic announcement and indicating the changes has not been accomplished.

Transitions and markers help to make your response more cohesive. In this response the phrase *Four activities* . . . clearly marks the transition from departure time to what is planned for the day. The rater is also clued in to specifically listen for four activities. Transitions like *From there we will drive* . . . , *This will be followed by* . . . , and . . . *our sight-seeing continues* . . . indicate a shift from one activity to the next. By using cohesive devices in your response you demonstrate fluency and control of language to the rater.

The announcement concludes with a statement that encourages the audience to participate in this upcoming event: *If you haven't signed up already, be sure to sign up today before you leave!* Encouraging participation demonstrates audience awareness.

An alternative approach to responding to this question would be to refer the audience to the printed schedule and focus on the changes as shown below.

Good afternoon, ladies and gentlemen of the Glenview Historical Society. You are all invited on our trip to Springfield. Please pull out your copies of the schedule so we can briefly review it together. There are four important changes that we all should be aware of.

First of all, our trip will take place on Friday, October 13th, not Thursday as was misprinted in the schedule. Please note that on your schedule.

Second, we will be taking the van from Jefferson Community College at 7:30 a.m., not 8:00 a.m. as printed. So don't come at 8:00 or you will miss the van! We have a full agenda of activities scheduled from 10 a.m. to 5 p.m. Please refer to your schedule for the details. I think you will particularly enjoy the noon demonstration at the Memorial Carillon.

The third change you should mark down is that we will be touring the Illinois State Capitol instead of the Illinois State Museum. The state museum will be closed for repairs; however, I know you will enjoy the capitol.

Finally, and best of all, is that the cost of the trip has been reduced from $5.00 to $3.00. Sign up today before you leave, if you haven't already done so.

A number of useful expressions for highlighting changes are summarized below.

instead	we changed
unfortunately	you should be aware
adjusted from __ to __	it was necessary to change
please note that	originally, . . . but now . . .
please make a note of it	

Exercise 7.2

In the exercise below you are given sets of words. The first is the original information; the second is the change. Think of three ways to express each change. Write out these changes in complete sentences and then say them aloud. The first one has been done for you.

1. leave 9:00 a.m./8:30

    - We will be leaving at 8:30 a.m., not 9:00 a.m. as originally scheduled.

    - Please make a note of the change in departure time. We will be leaving at 8:30 a.m., not 9:00.

    - In order to beat the traffic we will be leaving at 8:30 a.m. instead of 9:00.

2. take the bus/car pool

    _____

    _____

    _____

3. date Thursday May 17/Friday May 18

    _____

    _____

    _____

4. lunch at Allan's Steak House/the Vegetarian Cuisine

    _____

    _____

    _____

5.   entrance fee $20/$25

_____

_____

_____

7b. Announcement Section, Practice Questions

These practice questions will help you prepare to think quickly and respond
concisely to the types of questions found in the announcement section.
Work on one question at a time. If you preview all the questions at once,
you will ruin the spontaneity. Make your practice as realistic as possible by
not looking ahead at other questions and by keeping the time limit. For each
set of questions below, tape-record your responses. As you listen to your
recorded responses, see if you have clearly highlighted the changes in the
announcements and if you have appropriately addressed the intended
audience. Correct and repeat responses that need improvement.

Practice Set 1

- Let's pretend that you are the chairperson of the Greenville Botanical Society. Below you will see an agenda for an upcoming trip to the Botanical Gardens. As chairperson of the Greenville Botanical Society you have had the responsibility for planning this trip. You mailed a copy of the trip agenda to all the Greenville Botanical Society members four weeks ago. Since then, you noticed some errors and some last minute revisions. Pretend you are at the monthly meeting of the Greenville Botanical Society and you want to review the schedule of the trip with the other members and emphasize the corrections in the agenda. Because this is an oral presentation to the members of your organization you do not want to simply read the information printed on the agenda. Take the next 60 seconds to think about your presentation. On the actual test, you will hear the test narrator ask you to begin your presentation.
(response time = 90 seconds)

GREENVILLE BOTANICAL SOCIETY
Botanical Gardens Trip

Date:	Saturday, August ~~23~~ **24**	
Transportation:	Tourlines Bus Service	
Departure:	~~11:00~~ **10:45** a.m.	Park District Parking Lot B
Agenda:	12:00 p.m.	Lunch at the Garden Cafe
	1:30 p.m.	Tour Wildflower Gardens
	2:30 p.m.	Fields Auditorium
		Special Lecture on ~~Japanese Gardens~~ **Flower Arranging**
	3:30 p.m.	Guided Tour of Japanese Gardens
	4:15 p.m.	Guilford Tea Room
		Japanese Tea Ceremony*
Return:	5:30 p.m.	
Cost:	~~$12.00~~ **$15.00** per person (includes lunch and transportation)	

---

*No photographing permitted.

Practice Set 2

- Let's pretend that you are the social director for the Cosmopolitan Club. Below you will see an agenda for the 4th of July holiday. As social director of the Cosmopolitan Club you have had the responsibility of planning for this holiday. You just finished passing out a copy of this announcement to all the Cosmopolitan Club members at one of the regular meetings. Since this announcement was printed, you noticed some errors and some last minute revisions. Pretend you need to review the schedule with the other members and emphasize the corrections in the agenda. Because this is an oral presentation to the members of your organization you do not want to simply read the information printed on the agenda. Take the next 60 seconds to think about your presentation. On the actual test, you will hear the test narrator ask you to begin your presentation.
(response time = 90 seconds)

COSMOPOLITAN CLUB
July 4th Picnic

Date: Tuesday, July 4th

Parade: 1:00 p.m.   Main Street, ~~east side of Pine Grove~~ *between 3rd and 5th Street*

Barbecue: 3:30 p.m.   ~~Pine Grove~~ *Rotary* Picnic Shelter
Please bring:*   A–H   Side dish or chips
I–P   Salad
Q–Z   Dessert

Games: ~~5:00~~ *4:30* p.m.   Horseshoe contest
5:30 p.m.   ~~Volleyball Match~~ *Softball game*
6:00 p.m.   3-legged race, all age groups

Fireworks: 8:30 p.m. (or after dusk)
Norton Golf Course, north of Pine Grove

---

*Drinks, hamburgers, and table service provided.

Announcement for Practice Set 2

Practice Set 3

- Let's pretend that you are the president of the University Alumni Association. Below you will see an agenda for an upcoming trip to the university campus. As president of the University Alumni Association you have had the responsibility for planning this trip. You mailed a copy of the trip agenda to all the University Alumni members three weeks ago. Since then, you noticed some errors and some last minute revisions. Pretend you are at the monthly meeting of the University Alumni Association and you want to review the schedule of the trip with the other members and emphasize the corrections in the agenda. Because this is an oral presentation to the members of your organization you do not want to simply read the information printed on the agenda. Take the next 60 seconds to think about your presentation. On the actual test, you will hear the test narrator ask you to begin your presentation.

(response time = 90 seconds)

UNIVERSITY ALUMNI ASSOCIATION

Campus Visit

Date: Saturday, October ~~8~~ **12**

Breakfast: 8:15 a.m.   Breakfast at ~~University~~ **Roosevelt** Inn
                               Speaker: Prof. Atkins, Biological Sciences

Facilities Tour: 10:00 a.m.   William Hall Research Center
                               Tour guide: ~~Prof. Marsh~~ **Prof. Stevenson**, Computer Science

Lunch/Shopping: ~~11:30 a.m.~~ **12:00 p.m.**   Campus Town*

Concert: 3:30 p.m.   Smith Center for the Performing Arts
                               Concert Band led by Prof. Rogers, Music

Dinner: 6:30 p.m.   Grand Ballroom, Student Union
                               Dancing starting at 8:30 p.m.

---

*Lunch on your own.

Announcement for Practice Set 3

Practice Set 4

- Let's pretend that you are the instructor for a chemistry class. Below you will see a schedule for December, the last month of the fall term. As the instructor for the class you have had the responsibility for planning the syllabus. You just finished passing out a copy of the schedule to all the students in your class. Since the time you photocopied this schedule, you noticed some errors and some last minute revisions. Pretend it is the beginning of class and you want to review the schedule with your students and emphasize the corrections in the schedule. Because this is an oral presentation to the students in your class, you do not want to simply read the information printed on the schedule. Take the next 60 seconds to think about your presentation. On the actual test, you will hear the test narrator ask you to begin your presentation.
(response time = 90 seconds)

Chemistry 201
December Schedule

leave campus at 1:30 p.m.

Field Trip:	Friday, December 3
	Plymouth Pharmaceutical Labs
Lab Report 5:	Due Friday, December ~~9~~ 10
Midterm Exam:*	10:00 a.m. Monday, December 13
	open book, open notes
Final Review Session:	6:30 p.m., Wednesday, December 15
	212 ~~205~~ Chemistry Annex Building
Final Exam:*	~~1:30~~ 1:00 p.m., Saturday, December 18
	Van Huis Auditorium

---

*Programmable calculators not allowed.

Announcement for Practice Set 4

Practice Set 5

- Let's pretend that you are the instructor for an art class. Below you will see a schedule for a field trip to the art museum. As the instructor for the class you have had the responsibility for planning this field trip. You handed out a copy of the agenda to all your students at the last class meeting. Since then, you noticed some errors and some last minute revisions. Pretend it is the beginning of the next class and you want to review the agenda of the trip with your students and emphasize the corrections in the schedule. Because this is an oral presentation to the students in your class, you do not want to simply read the information printed on the schedule. Take the next 60 seconds to think about your presentation. On the actual test, you will hear the test narrator ask you to begin your presentation. (response time = 90 seconds)

ART 211

Museum Visit

Date:	Saturday, ~~March 27~~ April 4	
Departure:	9:30 a.m.	Bus leaves from the ~~north~~ west entrance of the Art & Design Building
Agenda:	11:00 a.m.	Guided tour of ~~European~~ American Exhibit
	12:30 p.m.	Lunch at the Watercolor Cafe*
	1:30 p.m.	Watkins Auditorium special lecture on Modern Art by ~~Harriett Shields, Director~~ Debbie Farrell, Assist Dir.
	2:30 p.m.	Guided tour of Egyptian Art Exhibit
	3:30 p.m.	Free time to view exhibits
Return:	~~5:00~~ 5:30 p.m.	Bus leaves from the main entrance to the Art Museum

*Bring money for lunch.

Announcement for Practice Set 5

Chapter 8
Final Notes

If you have worked your way to this point in this book, you have done some of the best preparation possible to maximize your performance on the TSE test and the SPEAK test. You are now familiar with test instructions, sample questions, time allotments, and the qualities that make good answers. Take advantage of the practice questions included at the end of each chapter. Sit down and record your answers to the practice questions in the time allotted for that type of question. Listen to your answers and check to see how well you do in comparison to the criteria discussed in this book. Practice until you are comfortable answering new questions in a fluent, coherent, comprehensible manner. Of course, actually speaking with native speakers of American English on a regular basis is a great way to improve your communication skills.

Health, stress, environment, and other factors can have an effect on your final test performance as well. Listed below are some general guidelines for taking tests. Many of these suggestions came from the Counseling Center at the University of Illinois.

Before the test

1. Get a good night's sleep.
2. Avoid taking stimulants to keep you up late the night before the test.
3. Allow ample time to get to the test site. If you don't know where the test site is, locate it prior to the test date.
4. Bring a magazine or book to read to keep you relaxed while you wait to be seated in the exam room.
5. Be positive about the test. Visualize yourself competently answering each question and push negative thoughts aside.
6. Ask the test proctor any questions you have before the test actually begins.
7. Don't wear noisy jewelry that could make distracting noises on your test recording.

8. Prepare for the test well in advance with this book and by speaking English as much as possible. Avoid cramming the night before the test.

During the test

9. Give your complete attention to each question. Don't become distracted by noise or other examinees.
10. Sit up straight during the test in order to breathe enough air to speak clearly.
11. Talk clearly into the microphone. Don't eat candy or put other things in your mouth that could detract from your speech. Keep your hands away from your mouth and face so you can be clearly recorded.
12. Listen to and read instructions carefully.
13. Bring a watch with a second hand or a digital watch that counts seconds in order to pace yourself through the test.
14. If there are any problems at all with the test equipment notify the test proctor immediately.
15. Don't leave any question unanswered. If you don't hear a question clearly, be sure to read it in the test book. If you are unsure of the meaning of a specific question, say so. Explain how you interpret the question and respond as best as you possibly can. Raters will rate the speech sample provided as best they can. If there is no response given or the simple response of *I don't know* or *I don't understand,* then that response will not receive many points.
16. Focus on performing the language functions required in each question, like giving directions, recommending, describing, defining, or persuading.

After the test

17. Don't discuss the details of the test; this may produce more anxiety for you.
18. Reward yourself by doing something you enjoy.
19. Remember, test scores do not set a value on your individual human worth!

Appendixes

Appendix A
Unofficial Practice Tests

The two practice tests in this appendix are similar to a TSE test or SPEAK test you may take; however, they should not be confused with real versions of the TSE test and SPEAK test designed by ETS. After completing this book, use these two tests for realistic practice of an entire test. Tape-record yourself and monitor your time. Evaluate your responses alone or with a friend based on the criteria of language function, coherence and cohesion, appropriateness, and accuracy as discussed in this book.

Practice Test 1

This test is designed to help you practice for the TSE test or SPEAK test.
Use a tape recorder to record your response to each question. There is a
time limit following each question. Use a watch and force yourself to
stick with these time limits. Do your best to answer as well as you can
within the stated time limits. The total test time is about twenty
minutes. These questions are not intended to measure your knowledge
of any particular field but to provide a context for your communicative
ability to be evaluated.

Remember to speak directly into your tape recorder. In order to
maximize your practice by creating a realistic testing situation, you
should not stop recording during the test.

This test begins with a few simple questions about familiar things. These are
warm-up questions to help you get ready for the main test questions.
However, your warm-up responses will not be listened to by the raters. Do
your best to give complete responses to each of these questions.

- What is the color of your test booklet?
  (response time = 10 seconds)
- How long does it take you to get ready in the morning?
  (response time = 10 seconds)
- Why did you last go shopping?
  (response time = 10 seconds)

That finishes the warm-up questions, and now on to the rated part of
the test. For each question, try to communicate your thoughts to the
rater in a complete and understandable manner.

For the next few questions try to pretend that you work at the new bookstore in town and that I came to shop here for the first time. Please look over the floor plan of the bookstore for the next half of a minute. After that you will be asked the questions written below.

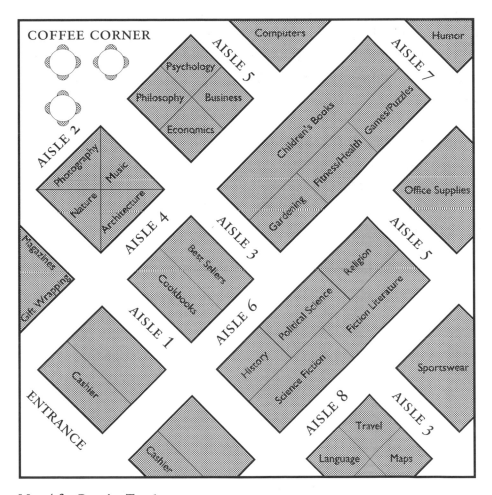

Map 4 for Practice Test 1

1. Decide on one section of the store you would like to look at. Tell me why this section is interesting to you.
   (response time = 30 seconds)
2. I wandered over to the map section. Now I would like to go to the coffee corner to have a cup of coffee while I study the map I picked out. Please tell me how to get from the map section to the coffee corner?
   (response time = 30 seconds)
3. I won a $50 gift certificate to this store. What would you recommend I buy? Please explain your reasons for recommending this purchase?
   (response time = 60 seconds)

In this section of the test you will see six pictures that depict a story line. You will be given 60 seconds to review the pictures. After that you will be asked to tell the short story that is illustrated by the pictures. Try to include all six pictures in your story. On the actual test, the test narrator will tell you when you may start telling the story.

4. Here are six pictures that illustrate a short story. Starting at the beginning, tell me the complete story picture by picture.
    (response time = 60 seconds)

5. In order to avoid this problem, what specific precautions do you think could have been taken?
    (response time = 30 seconds)

6. Let's pretend you are one of the people in the scene. This is the first warm weekend you have had all summer. However, before going to the beach you check the weather forecast and discover that there is a fifty percent chance of rain. Your friend wants to cancel the trip to the beach, but you don't. Role-play your discussion to convince your friend to go to the beach.
    (response time = 45 seconds)

7. Many national parks contain beautiful beaches and forests. People have varying opinions about whether national parks should be free for all citizens of that nation or if it is good to charge entrance fees. Pretend you are talking with a friend about the pros and cons of entrance fees for national parks.
    (response time = 60 seconds)

Pictures for Practice Test 1

The next few questions will ask you about your thoughts on a number of different issues. Feel free to think for a couple of seconds before you begin speaking. Try to answer as thoroughly as you can in the time given for each question.

8. Tenure is an employment system that guarantees teachers employment under certain conditions. However, people have varying opinions about tenure for teachers. Please tell me your opinion about this question.
    (response time = 60 seconds)

9. Imagine that I'm a friend who comes from a different country than you. Please define and explain cross-cultural communication for me.
    (response time = 60 seconds)

10. Illustrated here is a graph that shows the portion of the budget dedicated to education for one particular country. I am looking at this graph, but I need you to tell me about the data portrayed in it.
    (response time = 60 seconds)

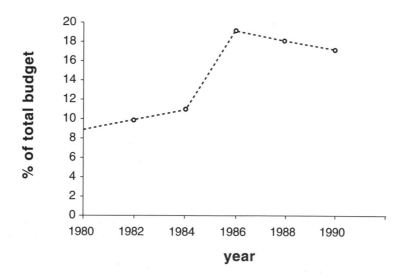

Government Allocations to Education

11. Please discuss how you think the budget for education could affect the future of the people in this country.
    (response time = 45 seconds)

12. Let's pretend that you are the personnel manager of the Pearson Group, Inc. On this page you will see an agenda for an upcoming orientation. As personnel manager of the Pearson Group, Inc., you have had the responsibility for planning this orientation. You just finished distributing a copy of the orientation agenda to all the new employees. Since then, you noticed some errors and some last minute revisions. Pretend you are at a business meeting with the new employees and you want to review the schedule of the orientation and emphasize the revisions in the agenda. Because this is an oral presentation to the members of your organization you do not want to simply read the information printed on the agenda. Take the next 60 seconds to think about your presentation. On the actual test, you will hear the test narrator ask you to begin your presentation.
(response time = 90 seconds)

PEARSON GROUP, INC.
New Employee Orientation*

Date:	Monday, January 5/ 6	
Welcome:	8:00 a.m.	Elizabeth Pearson, Pres.
Presentation 1:	8:30 a.m.	Alex Weldon, V.P. Finance ~~Sally Goldman, V.P. Manufacturing~~ Overview of company history
Coffee Break:	9:30 a.m.	
Video:	9:45 a.m.	Pearson: Building the Future Together
Presentation 2:	10:15 a.m.	Susan Hanson, H.R. Assistant Manager ~~Samuel Martin, Human Resources Manager~~ Overview of organizational chart
Presentation 3:	11:00 a.m.	Robert Elliot, V.P. Human Resources Understanding your employee benefits
Lunch:	12:30 ~~12:00~~ p.m.	Lunch catered by Arnold's

---

*Bring your company notebook with you.

Announcement for Practice Test 1

Practice Test 2

This test is designed to help you practice for the TSE test or SPEAK test. Use a tape recorder to record your response to each question. There is a time limit following each question. Use a watch and force yourself to stick with these time limits. Do your best to answer as well as you can within the stated time limits. The total test time is about twenty minutes. These questions are not intended to measure your knowledge of any particular field but to provide a context for your communicative ability to be evaluated.

Remember to speak directly into your tape recorder. In order to maximize your practice by creating a realistic testing situation, you should not stop recording during the test.

The test begins with a few simple questions about familiar things. These are warm-up questions to help you get ready for the main test questions. However, your warm-up responses will not be listened to by the raters. Do your best to give complete responses to each of these questions.

- What is your address?
  (response time = 10 seconds)
- How long does it take to travel from your home to the airport?
  (response time = 10 seconds)
- Why did you last use the telephone?
  (response time = 10 seconds)

That finishes the warm-up questions, and now on to the rated part of the test. For each question, try to communicate your thoughts to the rater in a complete and understandable manner.

For the next few questions try to pretend that we are classmates from college. We are looking at a map of your hometown together. Please look over the map for the next half of a minute. After that you will be asked the questions written below.

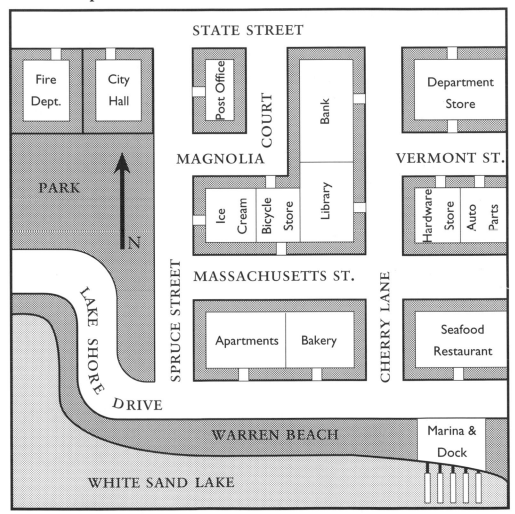

Map for Practice Test 2

1. The fire department gives seminars on fire safety. Suggest to me some things people can do to prevent fires?
   (response time = 30 seconds)
2. I need to meet another friend at the bakery. Please tell me how to get from the fire station to the bakery.
   (response time = 30 seconds)
3. You just came from the bakery. I'd like to know what your favorite dessert is. Tell me why you recommend it.
   (response time = 60 seconds)

In this section of the test you will see six pictures that depict a story line. You will be given 60 seconds to review the pictures. After that you will be asked to tell the short story that is illustrated by the pictures. Try to include all six pictures in your story. On the actual test, the test narrator will tell you when you may start telling the story.

4. Here are six pictures that illustrate a short story. Starting at the beginning, tell me the complete story picture by picture.
    (response time = 60 seconds)

5. In order to avoid this probblem, what specific precautions could have been taken?
    (response time = 30 seconds)

6. Let's pretend you are the postal worker in this scene. You have been continually bothered by dogs all summer long. Even though there is an abundance of employees working inside the post office and a lack of employees to work outside delivering the mail, you are determined to convince your supervisor to give you a job assignment where you can work inside the post office away from dogs. Role-play your discussion to convince your supervisor.
    (response time = 45 seconds)

7. The federal governments of many countries operate post offices. Some people have varying opinions about whether private industry or government should be responsible for the delivery of letters and packages. Pretend you are talking with your supervisor about the pros and cons of private industry operating mail service in a country.
    (response time = 60 seconds)

1

2

3

4

5

6

Pictures for Practice Test 2

The next few questions will ask you about your thoughts on a number of different issues. Feel free to think for a couple of seconds before you begin speaking. Try to answer as thoroughly as you can in the time given for each question.

8. People have varying opinions about whether TV is a good way for a person to learn a second language. Please tell me your opinion about this question.

   (response time = 60 seconds)

9. Imagine that I'm a beginning college student. Please define and explain the bachelor's, master's, and doctor's degrees.

   (response time = 60 seconds)

10. Illustrated here is a graph that shows the cost of road construction in a specific state. I am looking at the graph, but I need you to tell me about the data portrayed in it.

    (response time = 60 seconds)

Road Construction

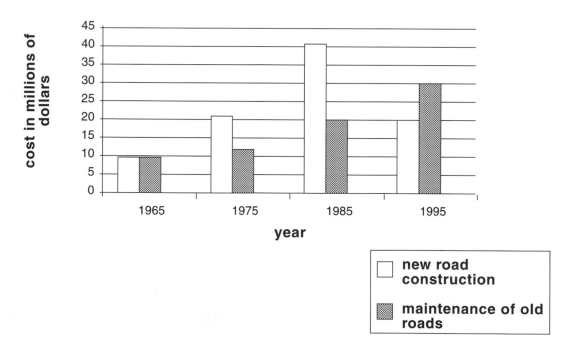

11. Please discuss how you think the cost of road construction could affect the future of the people in this state.

    (response time = 45 seconds)

12. Let's pretend that you are the president of the Alpha Service Fraternity. On this page you will see an agenda for an upcoming workday. As president of the Alpha Service Fraternity you have had the responsibility for planning this work day. Three weeks ago you mailed out a copy of the work day agenda to all the members of the Alpha Service Fraternity. Since then, there have been some last minute revisions. Pretend you are at a regular biweekly meeting with the other members and you want to review the schedule of the workday and emphasize the revisions in the agenda. Because this is an oral presentation to the members of your organization you do not want to simply read the information printed on the agenda. Take the next 60 seconds to think about your presentation. On the actual test, you will hear the test narrator tell you to begin your presentation.

(response time = 90 seconds)

ALPHA SERVICE FRATERNITY
Community Workday

Date: Saturday, April ~~14~~ 15
8:30 a.m. - 3:00 p.m.

Where: Ulysses S. Grant Park

Morning Projects: Scrape Fellows Field House
Paint Fellows Field House*
Repair old playground equipment /and install new swingset

Lunch: 12:00 p.m.   Picnic Lunch at ~~Greenfield~~ Fairfield Shelter

Afternoon Projects: Lay patio blocks
Plant shrubs and flowers — and 3 mapletrees
Install bike racks
Clean up litter

Dinner: ~~6:00~~ 6:30 p.m.   Appreciation dinner for all volunteers
at the Fellows Field House

*Bring your own painting tools.

Announcement for Practice Test 2

Appendix B
Test Registration Information

TSE Test

Educational Testing Services distributes free *TOEFL Bulletins* that contain information on TSE test dates as well as a TSE test registration form. These are frequently available at universities in the United States through the international student offices or English as a second language offices on campuses. To request a current *TOEFL Bulletin* directly from ETS you can contact Educational Testing Service by:

Phone: (609) 771-7100
Mail: TOEFL/TSE Services
Test of English as a Foreign Language
P.O. Box 6151
Princeton, NJ 08541-6151
E-mail: toefl@ets.org

Information is also available on the ETS web site:

http://www.toefl.org

SPEAK Test

SPEAK tests are given at many universities in the United States. Contact your department to find out who to talk to about the SPEAK testing program on your campus.

Bibliography

Dickerson, W., and L. Hahn. 1998. *Speechcraft: Discourse Pronunciation for Advanced Learners*. Ann Arbor, MI: University of Michigan Press.

Division of Measurement and Evaluation, University of Illinois. 1994. *Q & A*. fall, vol. 2, no. 1. Champaign–Urbana, IL.

———. 1995. *Q & A*. spring, vol. 2, no. 2. Champaign-Urbana, IL.

Educational Testing Service. 1995a. *TSE Score User's Manual*. Princeton, NJ: ETS.

———. 1995b. *TOEFL Bulletin 1995–96*. Princeton, NJ: ETS.

———. 1996. *SPEAK Rater Training Guide*. Princeton, NJ: ETS.

Hopkins, K. D., J. C. Stanley, and B. R. Hopkins. 1990. *Educational and Psychological Measurement and Evaluation*. Englewood Cliffs, NJ: Prentice-Hall.

Smith, J., C. M. Meyers, and A. J. Burkhalter. 1992. *Communicate: Strategies for International Teaching Assistants*. Englewood Cliffs, NJ: Regents/Prentice-Hall.

Wennerstrom, A. 1989. *Techniques for Teachers: A Guide for Nonnative Speakers of English*. Ann Arbor, MI: University of Michigan Press.